BE THE
TARGET

HOW TO LET GO AND
PLAY THE GAME OF GOLF

BYRON HUFF
FOREWORD BY BOB TOSKI

CONTEMPORARY BOOKS

A TRIBUNE NEW MEDIA/EDUCATION COMPANY

Library of Congress Cataloging-in-Publication Data

Huff, Byron.
    Be the target : how to let go and *play* the game of golf /
Byron Huff ; foreword by Bob Toski.
        p.   cm.
    ISBN 0-8092-3204-9
      1. Golf.   I. Title.
   GV965.H84   1996
   796.352—dc20   95-43152
                                                 CIP

Excerpt from *Golf in the Kingdom*, by Michael Murphy, page iii,
© 1972 by Michael Murphy, published by Viking Penguin, a
division of Penguin Books USA Inc.

Excerpt on page 21 reprinted with permission of Simon &
Schuster from *The Golf Swing*, by Cary Middlecoff. Copyright
© 1974 by Cary Middlecoff.

Photographs, photographic art, and illustrations by Byron Huff

Copyright © 1996 by Byron Huff
All rights reserved
Published by Contemporary Books, Inc.
Two Prudential Plaza, Chicago, Illinois 60601-6790
Manufactured in the United States of America
International Standard Book Number: 0-8092-3204-9
10   9   8   7   6   5   4   3   2   1

There are other myths to govern our lives, other impulses lurking in our soul, "myths of arrival with our myths of the journey, something to tell us we are the target as well as the arrow."

Michael Murphy
Golf in the Kingdom

This book is dedicated to my mother, Virginia Huff, for her tireless dedication to her family and friends, and to Isidoro Baltazar, for passing on his knowledge.

Contents

Acknowledgments

This book has been a labor of love. The friendship and inspiration of many people helped make it possible.

My thanks go to James Huff, Bob Toski, Roger Schiffman, June Crabtree, Nancy Crossman, Tony Manzanares, Marilyn Peek, Sam Pinkus, Ellen Ruckel, and Don Wade.

And thank you to Mariano Aureliano, Kim Bartko, Frank Barylski, Brian Bergstrom, Charles Bolling, Craig Bolt, Nathan Brandimarte, Gordon Campbell, Robert Carney, Mary Higgins Clark, Steve Cohen, Alina Cowden, Mike Diffley, Martha Farris, Marie Fischer, Barbara Hearst, Susan Hendry, Gary Jobe, Leslie McNew, Michael Murphy, Kevin O'Malley, Thomas Quick, Jennifer Schultheis, Fred Shoemaker, Chip Smith, George Stavropoulis, Bob Stutts, Tom Sullivan, Hugh White, and Sal Zaccagnino.

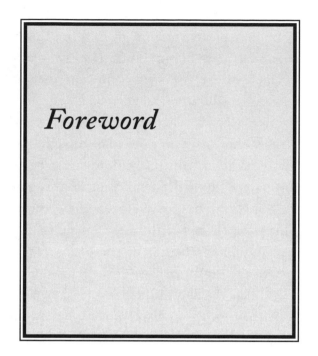

Foreword

I am very pleased and happy to write this foreword for my good friend Byron Huff. His awareness to the basic instincts of the golf swing and how they are performed is refreshing, educational, and sound.

Byron has touched on many subjects in this book that many authors have overlooked or thought not important. He has brought to light many things that beginners and good players need to understand to make this game enjoyable.

Simplicity has always been the answer to complexity. This book clears a path in the jungle so the golfer can see, feel, and know where he is going.

All great players have great imagination and great feel. They plan the shot, visualize the shot, and execute. They trust their swing! Poor players are bound up in mechanical thoughts. Their swings are contrived—meaning that they try to effect a result by manipulating the club during the swing. One cannot play golf effectively this way! Most golfers try to, however, and are in their own way. *Be the Target* will open your eyes, clear your mind, and help your mind and body become one in the act of producing a golf swing that is more effective and consistent.

The hit is a result of the ball getting in the way of the swinging club. Most golfers play just the opposite way. Byron has taught the golfer to eliminate the "hit" syndrome!

One of the most important things Byron has addressed in this book is the subject of slow play. The courses are cluttered with golfers holding up play because they are not prepared to play the game as he proposes. The "fear of failure" must be eliminated. A more positive approach is needed; this book is an antidote for despair.

This book is so different and refreshing. Knowing Byron for all these years makes me feel proud and happy that he has undertaken this great task.

He has learned his lessons well, and taken many steps forward for the benefit of all golfers in this great game.

May you heed the wisdom of his words.

                                                        Bob Toski

Preface

The essence of this book is revealed in the words "Golf is an art, not a science." *Be the Target* is designed to enable golfers to free their minds of scientific, analytical swing thoughts on the course and develop a swing that instinctively reacts to the target.

Golfing instincts—that is, your reactive "feel" for the game—can be difficult to further define in words because they are borne of the subconscious, whereas words are in the realm of the conscious mind. However, these instincts can be learned and enhanced through the exercises presented in the following pages.

Like most youngsters, I learned to play golf in an instinctive way, with hardly a thought as to how I was doing it. In high school I was around a 5 handicap, runner-up in the sectional championships, and a player in the Metropolitan Amateur. Decent, but nothing special. And it wasn't long before I, like many others, became preoccupied with swing mechanics.

I crossed paths with Bob Toski in the mid-1970s. It was a wonderful time, not least because I learned so much from him. In particular, I recall a class he taught at the Hidden Valley Golf Club in Miami, Florida. I was one of about fifteen students to whom he posed the question, "What determines the length of your backswing?" At first, we were all silent. Then someone blurted out, "The length of your shoulder turn!" Bob shook his head. Someone else declared, "The amount of flex in your right knee!" Others said, "The amount of your wrist cock"; "how straight you keep your left arm"; and, "the distance your hips turn." People kept shouting answers and Bob just kept shaking his head. We were all so preoccupied with swing mechanics that we had lost sight of the objective of a golf shot, and Bob was trying to rescue us. Finally, he gave us the answer: "The length of the backswing is determined by the distance you have to strike the ball to your target." So very simple, and implying so much about golfing feel and instinct—and yet, no one in the group got it until he told us. I believe to this day that a majority of golfers still don't make this connection on the golf course.

A few years ago I had the privilege of attending a couple of seminars at the Esalen Institute in California that were loosely based on the book *Golf in the Kingdom* by Michael Murphy and The School for Extraordinary Golf run by Fred Shoemaker, co-leader of the seminars. The other leaders were Steve Cohen, who contributed his knowledge of exploring the "inner self" through principles of meditation and gestalt, and Brian Bergstrom, who shared his knowledge of yoga, stretching, and other body work. By focusing on the sources of frustration and anxiety in golfers (and people in general), they have fashioned an environment conducive to the learning and development of the golfing instincts, one that fosters the trust and confidence needed to let go and play. My hat is off to them all. They have truly been an inspiration, and I strongly recommend any and all to go and work with them.

It is my contention that a preoccupation with swing mechanics on the golf course not only leads to frustration and inconsistent shotmaking but is also the chief cause of slow play in the game as it is played at American clubs and courses. I've heard it said many times that the main reason for slow play was the imitating of tour players on TV as they take long periods of time to study their shots and get ready to play, especially in the dramatic later stages of a tournament. The reasoning is that if the tour players need to take a long time in order to play fine shots and shoot low scores, then amateurs should take just as long to achieve the same results. I disagree with this notion. I believe that golfers who imitate the studied play of the tour pros are merely looking for an excuse to take longer. Because most amateurs think mechanical thoughts while playing, the resulting confusion stirring just beneath the surface makes them fearful of pulling the trigger. They will now use any reason to delay the shot, and the best reason is to mimic the speed of play of the pros on TV.

For example, it has been shown that a foursome will tend to maintain for the entire round the pace it established on the first hole. Since most golfers initiate mechanical swing thoughts on the first tee due to nervousness, the first hole is almost always played slowly, setting the tone for the remaining holes.

Of course, there are other reasons for slow play, such as a lack of awareness of the *need* to keep things moving at a good pace, not being ready to play when it's your turn, modern "do-or-die" architecture with hazards everywhere and extremely undulating greens, unfamiliarity with the rules, and excessively long grass close to fast greens. All of these factors contribute to the general *inability* of a growing number of golfers to find their ball, play their shot, and find their ball again without delay. However, by studying the principles featured in this book and diligently practicing the exercises, you will increase your speed of play and enhance your enjoyment of the game as well.

This book will have the most immediate benefits for golfers who play and practice fairly frequently and can regularly break 100. Such golfers are already finding the ball with the clubface quite consistently, and have most likely developed a good degree of feel for some of the mechanics of the swing. However, I heartily recommend this book to all golfers aspiring to improve their game. It will heighten your awareness of *feel* and *instinct* in the golf swing and light the way for the time when you will transcend mechanical thoughts on the course and thereby increase your speed of play.

I wish to give golfers a simple manual by which they can discover their true golfing instincts (if they haven't already done so) and a quick reference and reminder should their golf-playing focus waver. I am not really saying anything new here, but I am attempting to organize things I've learned over the past thirty years in order to focus on the actual *playing* of golf more directly, yet more simply, than what's been published to date. Whether I've accomplished that is not for me to determine, but I can tell you from my experience, and the experiences that others have shared with me, that everything I've said here is true.

PART I

The Foundation

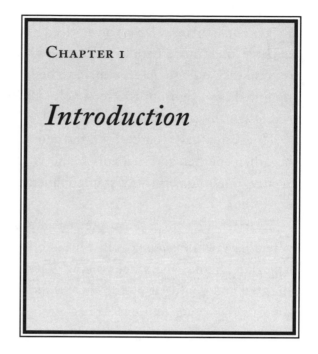

CHAPTER 1

Introduction

How many times have you noticed golfers on the first tee, their mood enthusiastic and jovial, their demeanor free and easy, only to observe them to be frustrated and disappointed two, eight, or fourteen holes later?

How many times has this happened to you?

How often have you been on the course and hit one bad shot, then another, and suddenly found yourself emotionally on edge, thinking negatively, your confidence gone, and ready to give up?

Everywhere I go I sense the tensions and frustrations golfers have while *playing* golf. Through individual lessons, magazines, books, and videos, many golfers have been both educated and confused by the sheer volume of analysis devoted to the swing motion. Armed with these thoughts of swing mechanics, perhaps the latest tip or the newest method, golfers actively try to manipulate their body and the club during the swing in order to "hit" the ball. The results of this *hit impulse* are nearly always frustrating and inconsistent. On the practice tee, where golfers can strike ball after ball, mechanical thoughts may work fine, but the on-course pressure of scoring leaves these players mired in their analyses and stuck playing well below their potential. So what do they do?

They seek out new tips, new methods, anything that will help; but their constant on-course analysis and over-control only increases their frustration and raises their score. Their golfing self-esteem begins to drop, along with their enjoyment of the game. It's an immense compliment to the game of golf that these golfers keep coming back for more, but the truth is, there is a much better way.

Picture this: You're on the golf course and you're enjoying yourself. It's actually becoming exciting. You're free of worry and frustration. In between shots, instead of talking to yourself and worrying about your swing, you're having a great time getting to know your playing partners and savoring the fresh air and scenery. When you step up to your shots there's an entirely different air about you. Gone are the fears and anxieties that have plagued you for so long, replaced by a calmness and trust in your golfing potential. Best of all, many of your shots are heading straight for the hole in a way you never thought possible when you began this amazing game.

Sound like wishful thinking? Well, it can be more than just that—a whole lot more. Through diligent application of the principles and exercises outlined in this book, you can turn this fantasy of a marvelous day of golf into a reality.

In this book you'll explore the difference between playing golf and practicing golf, as well as how, when, and where to do each. You'll begin to focus on *where* you want the ball to go rather than *how* to make it go there. By learning to let go of mechanical swing thoughts, and applying exercises designed to enhance your awareness of the target, you'll learn to develop a *swing instinct* instead of a *hit impulse* on the course. As you become more proficient at maintaining an awareness of the target throughout the entire swing, you'll become more adept at relinquishing conscious control of the club and trusting your swing to instinctively react to your awareness of the target. You'll discover how this creates an environment devoid of fear and frustration—just like the fantasy situation described earlier—and you'll develop the kind of free-flowing, full-motion swing you've always wanted. Since your focus will be much simpler, the result will be a more confident, anxiety-free execution of your shots.

In short, you'll learn how to shift your on-course golf-playing emphasis *from* thinking about mechanics and how to make a good swing at the ball *to* where you want the ball to go and a feel for reacting to the target. This will result in more consistent shotmaking and improved scores.

In addition, you'll be able to take your game from the practice tee to the first tee with no change in your ability to strike good golf shots, avoiding the inherent pitfalls most golfers encounter. And it will all serve to brighten your outlook and increase your golfing enjoyment.

Be the Target is different in two respects from most golf books.

Number one, the primary emphasis of this book is to define what it means to *play* golf versus what it means to *practice* golf. First, I explain how to approach the game on the course, and then how and where to practice. After all, playing the course is the goal of every golfer, and it is only by knowing what it means to play golf that you can truly understand how you should practice. My approach is the exact opposite of that found in most golf instructional books. Such books generally devote the first hundred and fifty or so pages entirely to practicing golf, by breaking down the swing into parts and explaining all of the various swing mechanics. Then, somewhere near the end, the reader—if he or she ever gets that far—will be told that, oh, by the way, you shouldn't think about mechanics while playing on the golf course! By this time, however, it's too late for average golfers to forget about mechanics. Their impressionable minds are already overloaded with information and, since the differences between playing and practicing golf haven't been emphasized from the beginning, they end up taking these mechanics out on to the course while playing. As a result they become "bound" to the ball instead of the target and develop the *hit* impulse, which leads to frustration, anxiety, and disappointment.

Number two is the simplicity of *Be the Target*. Most golfers are very sensitive creatures when it comes to learning swing mechanics—the mere mention of the term can jump-start the average golfer's mind. A book with a couple hundred pages on the subject can leave them lost in a quagmire of wordiness and in a state of "paralysis from analysis." This book, on the other hand, does away with such complexity and is designed to take a golfer's game to the course in a simple, easily digested fashion, making it eminently readable for all golfers.

Now let's look at how the information in this book is presented. Because so many golfers analyze their swings while playing, you'll begin with a chapter on why thinking about mechanics on the golf course doesn't work, a concept that is key to understanding the difference between playing and practicing golf.

Next you'll investigate how to play golf. You'll begin by learning how to determine your targets according to the principles of course management; then you'll learn to sense the components of the target picture and the proper "swing feel" needed to react to the target. Next, you'll find out how to maintain an awareness of the target picture throughout your entire swing. This will foster the trust necessary to allow your subconscious to properly react to the target picture. Then you'll discover how to solidify what you've learned by creating your own shot routine, the final step in putting it all together and playing golf with target awareness.

And last, you'll find out how to practice golf, including when to incorporate swing mechanics into your practice and when not to, and how to sense, or visualize, the execution of a successful golf shot in your mind.

This book is designed for players at all levels of golfing ability, from beginner to expert. At the very least, however, you must be able to consistently find the ball with the clubface on every swing. If that's the case, you probably have a handicap of around 24 or less. If your handicap is 25 or higher, after reading this book it is recommended that you concentrate on Part III, entitled "Practicing Golf" until your handicap gets a little lower. Which is not to say you can't begin applying the principles discussed in this book or perform the associated exercises. On the contrary, doing so can only further your understanding of the game and help you to establish and achieve your goals. However, you may not have as much success as you'd like (when you let go of thinking about mechanics on the course) until you have mastered some of the fundamental swing mechanics *on the practice tee* and ingrained them deeper in your subconscious.

The following chart was prepared to help you choose a course of action best suited to your particular golfing ability. This will enable you to obtain the maximum benefit from this book and more clearly focus on what you need to do to achieve golfing success.

And now, let's go find some of that wonderful golfing enjoyment!

Your Handi-cap	Chart for best success in using this book
	Comments
8 or less	Definitely into playing good golf. May visit the practice tee fairly regularly. Strong desire, good athletic ability and hand-to-eye coordination. You are ready to play target-oriented golf. Do you still think mechanics on the course? Do you have a *consistent* shot routine? Do you think about mechanics as you're warming up? Can you gauge the quality of your target awareness? Your *swing* instinct?
9 to 16	Shows a strong desire to be a better player. Good athletic ability and hand-to-eye coordination. Will enjoy this book combined with more regular practice. Have you ever played a round without thinking swing mechanics? Do you have a shot routine? Do you warm up before a round? How often do you practice your short game? Are you more focused on the ball or the target? How well do you finish your swing?
17 to 24	Definitely a golfer with ability, but could acquire added consistency by visiting the practice tee more often. This book can help to open your eyes. Do you practice mechanics on the lesson tee and carry them out to the course? How often do you get qualified PGA instruction? Practice more frequently, stay aware of your grip pressure, and use this book to understand what it means to be able to trust your swing.
25+	This book will help you set your goals and understand how to progress to the next level. Need to ingrain the fundamentals more deeply into the subconscious by doing some diligent work on the practice tee combined with professional instruction. Read on, and try the exercises—just don't expect too much in the beginning. Start now to develop a *swing* instinct and an awareness of your target picture.

CHAPTER 2

Swing Mechanics, and Why They Don't Work on the Golf Course

Golfers who worry about swing mechanics or analyze different facets of their swing while on the course are not really playing golf—they are just *practicing*.

To better understand why mechanical thinking doesn't work while playing, let's investigate why golfers think about swing mechanics on the golf course.

First, down through the history of golf instruction there has been an enormous emphasis on swing mechanics, and for very good reason. When golfers take up the game, they must devise a way to consistently find the ball with the clubface. In most other sports we look at the target: for example, in basketball we look at the rim when we shoot, and in baseball we look at the catcher's glove when we pitch. But in golf we look at the ball instead of the target, so the tendency is to focus on the ball. Hence, golfers make themselves available to the prodigious amounts of mechanical swing information found in books, magazines, videos, and supervised lessons, with their goal being to "hit" the ball correctly. As a result, either they never learn to consistently find the ball with the clubface or they become fascinated, and eventually quite preoccupied, with swing mechanics and develop an analytical "practice tee" mentality. Consequently, *they never get beyond thinking about swing mechanics.* They become oblivious to any advice telling them not to think about mechanics while playing.

Second, many golfers who have learned the mechanics of the swing sufficiently to be able to consistently find the ball with the clubface never come in contact with the knowledge needed to entrust the swing to their subconscious. There are very few books, magazines, videos, and teachers who expose golfers to anything other than swing mechanics, so many golfers never get the chance to learn how to let go of their analyses and just *play*. Swing mechanics are all they know, and that's what they go with.

Third, the practice tee, where one should study and learn swing mechanics, is a place most golfers seldom visit. They either don't have the time to practice or don't take the time. And many who visit the practice areas use them incorrectly and are unaware of the different ways there are to practice. As a result, golfers use the course rather than the practice tee to learn swing mechanics.

Fourth, tension in the arms and shoulders, as well as excessive grip pressure, will curtail a golfer's *swing* instinct and lead him down the path of mechanical swing thoughts. This is especially the case if he's playing in front of friends and fellow club members, or in adverse conditions such as strong winds.

Fifth, many golfers get trapped by the desire to have a "good-looking" swing instead of one that gets the job done: that is, getting the ball in the hole. Because these golfers are forever analyzing the different positions of their swing, they never fully develop the "whole" swing.

Still others keep thinking about mechanics because they're looking for that magic method, that secret tip that will get them to the promised land of a perfect swing!

These are some of the reasons why golfers analyze their

swings as they play. For such golfers, the spot where they want their ball to end up—the target—becomes and remains secondary to the goal of "hitting the ball."

Now let's take a look at what's wrong with this type of thinking on the course—how it hurts the golfer's game, causes mental frustration, and slows down the speed of play.

When golfers are thinking about mechanics during the swing, they generally concern themselves with those swing actions that take place prior to impact. This focuses their attention on the ball. This is called becoming *ball bound.* Being ball bound activates the *hit* impulse, which leads to golfers deliberately increasing their grip pressure on the downswing in order to manipulate the club in a particular way to "hit" the ball.

In his book *The Touch System for Better Golf,* Bob Toski explains, "Something in the human sensory system makes us hit *at* objects. And whenever we hit at something, the normal subconscious tendency is to slow down our hands and 'guide' them toward the object."

In his book *Shape Your Swing the Modern Way,* Byron Nelson says, "Whenever you consciously try to hit the ball on the downswing, to pour on the power in the impact area, you will inevitably do it too early."

Hence, by trying to "guide" the swing we tend to increase our grip pressure too early in the downswing. This causes our wrists to uncock prematurely, thus spoiling the shot. Nelson goes on to say, "It is humanly impossible to deliberately accelerate the clubhead into the ball on a full shot." In fact, all we do when we try to "hit" the ball on the down-

The pre-impact part of the swing, the part with which a "ball-bound" golfer is concerned

swing is impede the flow of our arm swing through the ball, which disrupts our timing, curtails the follow-through, and invariably ruins the shot.

Once golfers become *ball* bound, they leave themselves open to the dangers of the *hit* impulse. Any time ball-bound golfers are in a situation where tension might cause their grip pressure to increase—for example, when they're thinking about swing mechanics, playing from the first tee in front of several people, facing a "tight" lie, playing in the wind or rain, or in a pressure-filled match—they will invariably suc-

*An example of how
attempting to "hit" the
ball on the downswing
can uncock a golfer's wrists
too early*

cumb to the *hit* impulse and strike a poor shot. *The solution,
as you shall see, is to become "target bound," and play golf with
a "swing instinct."*

Many golfers fall into a trap I call the "cycle of unful-
filled expectations." Sometime previously, by luck or what
have you, a golfer will have shot an unusually low score. The
golfer may not realize it at this point, but a certain level of
expectation has been set and, human nature being what it is,
the golfer's sensitive psyche will settle for nothing less than
equally low scores on subsequent outings. When the golfer
fails to maintain the high standard of play, the pressure of
these expectations causes tension to slowly creep into the

swing. The golfer now starts to analyze the swing in greater detail and study any tip, technique, or mechanic that may improve it. All the while, the *hit* impulse within the golfer grows, fueled by the increasing on-course analysis which draws the attention more and more to the ball. The shot making becomes more inconsistent, scores rise and tension increases, leading to more analysis—and the cycle continues. Quite naturally, these tensions and frustrations slowly weigh on golfer's minds and diminish their enjoyment of the game.

As I stated earlier, I feel that this preoccupation with swing mechanics while playing is nearly universal, and it is one of the main reasons for the single worst problem in the game: slow play. The on-course pressure of scoring and the paralysis caused by too much analysis prevents the golfer from feeling the freedom, confidence, and trust needed to just let go and swing. Look how fast Bobby Jones and the players of yesterday went around the course. Jones himself often said words to the effect that the less he thought about his swing, the better he figured he could play.

Fred Shoemaker, who created the School for Extraordinary Golf, maintains that the thing a golfer fears most when he hits a bad shot is hitting *another* bad shot. If this is true— and I believe it is—then this places almost every golfer little more than two bad swings away from profound emotional distress. So it's only to be expected that, with fears like this running through golfers' minds, they have a difficult time pulling the trigger.

As you will see, an awareness of the target and the development of a *swing* instinct will alleviate the fears caused by "paralysis from analysis." And you will discover how the creation of a shot routine will give you a way to start the swing in the same fashion every time. And it is this combination of target awareness and a shot routine that allows for faster play and more enjoyable golf.

You have read why golfers think about swing mechanics on the course and the negative ways it affects them. Next you will take a look at the solutions to these problems and find the freedom and confidence necessary to trust your golf swing and find true golf-playing enjoyment.

PART II

Playing Golf

Now you'll examine how to play golf with target awareness. Swing mechanics will not be mentioned here.
You are going to learn to develop a swing that *instinctively*
reacts to the target.

Why should you become target-oriented on the golf
course? Why should you be sensing the target when you
swing? The target picture gives the swing something to
relate to. It provides the swing with an intended flight path
for the ball, giving the swing a definite path, the clubface a
specific direction, the backswing a certain length, and the
whole swing a certain pace. In short, the target picture gives
the swing its purpose, its goal. It gives the swing something
to react to. And, *it is the simplest way to play a golf shot.*

In my opinion, the best players in the world, meaning the
tour professionals, top club professionals, and top amateurs,
all play with a keen sense of target awareness. Some of them
may not realize this because they have probably been playing this way since day one. However, I don't believe these
players would be able to play the way they do, hit it as consistently close to the flag as they do, without maintaining a
very good target sense throughout their entire swing.

In his column in a 1989 issue of *Golf Digest*, Charles
Price recounted Bobby Jones's response to his question about
what Jones relied on to bring off a shot he needed to make
in a golf tournament. Jones answered, "Instincts. Instincts I
honed after practice combined with playing. The more I
depended on those instincts—the more I kept conscious
control out of mind—the more nearly the shot came off the
way I visualized it. Concentrating on the results of a shot to

the absolute exclusion of all other thoughts, especially about its method, *is the secret to every good shot I ever hit.*" Jones goes on to say, "The ability to play the shot you visualized and let trouble take care of itself is a rare quality in a golfer, one the average player should strive for more than perfection in a swing that may be beyond his capabilities anyway." The immortal Bobby also concluded, "I say from experience that 'choking' is caused by not using your own instincts."

The great Ben Hogan, thought of by some as a technical and quite mechanically minded golfer, actually was very target-oriented on the course. In his book *The Golf Swing*, Cary Middlecoff relates a conversation Hogan had with someone who wanted to know exactly what he was thinking just before he started his swing.

"All I think about *is trying to knock the ball in the hole*," said Hogan.

"Oh," said his questioner. "I thought maybe you used some sort of mental gimmick like starting the club back with your hands, or staying in the backswing plane, or something like that."

"No," said Hogan. "You have to work all that stuff out on the practice tee."

You'll begin this section by studying how to navigate your way around the course; that is, how to determine your targets with smart, sensible thinking. This is known as course management, and you'll briefly examine some of its principles.

Then you'll take a look at the target picture and learn to sense its various components.

Following that, you'll learn to develop a sense for the proper swing feel needed to react to the target picture.

Next, you'll discover how to maintain your sense of the target picture throughout the entire swing, fostering the trust necessary to allow yourself to instinctively react to that target picture and let the proper swing happen.

Then, you'll learn how to approach and execute every shot consistently by creating your own shot routine. This is the foundation for playing good golf, especially when the "heat is on."

Lastly, you'll take what you've learned to the course, where you'll *play* the game of golf with target awareness.

Learning to play golf with target awareness emphasizes being aware. That means being cognizant of what's going on inside of you (such as what you're feeling when you swing) and outside of you (such as the wind or your lie). It means keeping a quiet mind and just watching, feeling, and sensing. By doing this, you'll build up a storehouse of knowledge in your subconscious, thus fueling your instinctive feel for a golf shot. As you go through the following chapters, just try to observe and be aware of what you see and feel, and stay relaxed, keeping your mind as peaceful and quiet as you can.

CHAPTER 3

Determining Your Target

When you play golf, how often do you find your ball in play? Are you a regular visitor to the trees, the rough, the bunkers, the water? Do you go for the long distance off the tee, or do you keep a little power "in your pocket," sacrificing distance in order to have a shot from the fairway? Do you always shoot for the flag?

Course management is an often overlooked part of amateur golf, but it's the starting point on the road to lower scores through target awareness. Simply, your target should be a place that offers the best spot from which to play your next shot but which will hurt you the least if the shot does not come off as planned.

To accurately determine your target, you must come to know the strengths and weaknesses of your game and what you're capable of under various playing conditions such as a strong wind or a closely played match. You must be able to correctly diagnose the level of your shotmaking on that particular day, and, if you're playing a match, ascertain exactly how you stand.

How good is your short game? Are you a good bunker player? If so, maybe you can go for a pin that's tucked behind a bunker because you know that if you miss, you're still likely to get up and down. This is the way you must think yourself around the course. It's a method that will pay large dividends. You'll have significantly fewer penalty shots; as a result, you'll always be in the match.

Picking the best target can be really difficult if your ego demands that you strike the ball as far as you can, especially off the tee. Most golfers with a driver in their hands haven't picked a target; they just try to rip the ball as far as they can in a certain direction. Consequently, their shots go all over the place. The amazing thing about this is, if you hold back, sacrificing some distance in favor of a smoother, better-paced swing, the ball will often go farther and straighter than you ever imagined!

Map Your Layout and Chart Your Last Round

First find a map of the course's layout. The place mats in the grill room of your club may have the layout printed on them, or you may be able to obtain the layout from your scorecard and enlarge it on a copying machine. In the absence of a

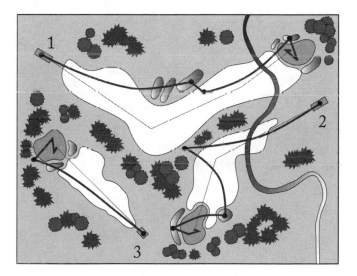

Section of a shot chart from a recent round

printed piece, draw a very simple picture of each hole on a sheet of paper, then make copies of it. On the first copy, chart the exact route you took on your last round.

Create a New Chart Using Course Management

Next, on another copy, select and mark your targets for every shot on every hole. As you select each one, be sure you have an excellent chance of hitting the target, even if it means sacrificing quite a bit of distance to keep the ball in play. Take into account the positions of the bunkers, water, trees, rough, and out-of-bounds, as well as your knowledge about your

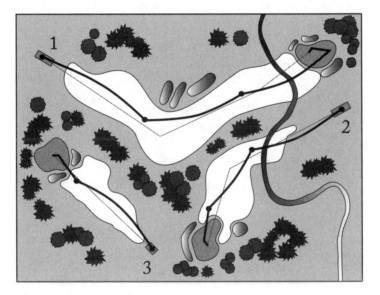

Section of a potential shot chart using course management

game, including short-game ability. Compare the two maps, noting their differences. Especially note which parts of your game now come more into play and which are de-emphasized. This will assist you later on in determining which shots you'll emphasize in practice.

Memorize the New Chart

Now, with the second map in hand, start on the first hole and mentally go through all eighteen holes, visualizing the ball flight of each shot going to the specified target. Be sure to go through all eighteen holes smoothly, without stopping. Do it again, if necessary, and keep doing it until you have committed all the targets to memory.

Play Eighteen Holes with Your New Targets

The next time you play a round of golf, aim for these targets and, no matter what, stick to your game plan. *Notice how you feel after the round*. I think you'll be surprised by how much you enjoyed playing and by the quality of your score. The secret to your success is being realistic about your target choices.

As you get better at golf and at course management, you'll be able to sense your targets as you are playing. But keeping everything in play should be your first goal. Once you're able to do that, then move on.

CHAPTER 4

Sensing the Target Picture

Using the principles of course management, you have now selected a proper place for your ball to finish. This is your target, and it is the star component in a larger scene called the *target picture*. To view the target picture, stand behind the ball and observe the scene before you.

The six components of the target picture. The first five components—the target, the terrain around the target, the wind, the lie, and the slope of the stance—determine the sixth component—the ball flight path.

On any shot, from a drive to a putt, there are six components to the target picture. The first five are the target, the
terrain around the target, the wind, the lie, and the slope of
the stance. (Obviously, the wind, the lie, and the slope of the
stance will probably have less influence on a putt than on a
full shot, but depending on where you're playing and the
conditions, they may still be a factor.) Together, except on
trouble shots,* these five components create, or *induce* in
your mind, the sixth component—the path your ball will
take to the target, or simply, the *ball flight path*.

This is very important, because by sensing the ball flight
path, you will then be able to sense the proper swing feel
necessary to react to that target picture and select the club
you will use. Jack Nicklaus has concluded that creating a
mental picture of a shot, which includes sensing the target
picture and the swing needed to react to that picture, is 50
percent of any golf shot. Fifty percent! That is how important sensing the target picture is.

The first goal of this chapter is to get the reader on the
road to becoming aware, instinctively aware, of the first five
components of the target picture. To be instinctively aware
means that you will develop an inherent feel, or sense, of each
component of the target picture and how that component
will affect the sixth component, the ball flight path.

---

*those shots that require a change in the length and/or direction of
your swing, or the path of your intended ball flight, due to an immediate obstacle or a very unusual stance or situation

1. The Target

Since the target is the goal of the shot, all we have to do here is simply look at it. However, there are different ways of looking at things, as the following exercises will demonstrate.

Check your target sense

First, just look at a target, or any object farther than, say, fifteen feet away. Really take a good look at it; see it the way an artist might, noticing its lines and colors, its shadows and highlights. Now, look away so it's no longer in your field of vision, including the periphery. Do you still know precisely where it is? Or do you feel a little vague and uncertain about its location? If the latter, look back and find it, then look away again. Better this time? Try again. This time, close your eyes and point to where you think the target is, then open your eyes and see how close you came. And notice how, after doing this a few times, you can improve your sense of where an object is without having to look directly at it.

How well developed is your sense of direction? Do you always have to consult a map when you are traveling through unfamiliar territory or need to find out which way is north? When, as a child, you played pin-the-tail-on-the-donkey, were you any good at it?

Look at everything but the target

Next, if you are outdoors, select a target about fifty yards away—a flagstick or a tree will do. If you are indoors, select an object on the other side of the room. Instead of looking directly at the target to the exclusion of everything else, try looking at everything *but* the target. Feel how your eyes are able to notice everything in your field of vision surrounding the target. You're not looking at anything specifically, rather you're taking in the whole scene around the target, including the periphery. You may find this easier to do if you relax your eyes and let them go slightly out of focus. The important thing is to realize that when you focus on a single object you may not see the whole picture, but when you look at everything *except* that object, you can sense the whole picture *and* the object. Paradoxically, you are more aware of the object because it is the only thing you're *not* looking at.

The following six pictures show the target from both perspectives. Do you notice any difference? Do some pictures give you more information about the shot than others?

Comparisons: seeing only *the target vs. everything* but *the target*

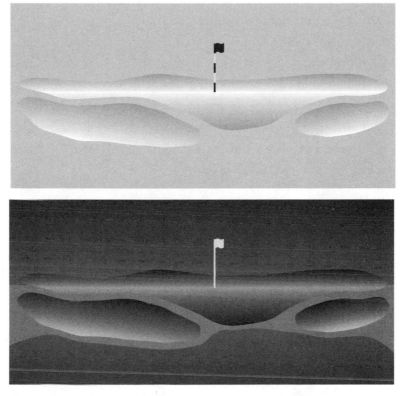

Comparisons: seeing only *the target vs. everything* but *the target*

If a target is very far away, say over 175 yards, some people may have a difficult time sensing how far that is, even when the exact yardage is displayed on a sprinkler head or the like. There's no question that we've become too reliant on yardage markers and course maps. How good are you at sensing yardage? Without markers can you tell when you are 125 yards from something? 150? 175? Ever notice how 100 yards seems much shorter on a golf course than a football field?

Check your depth awareness at different distances

Go out on the course when nobody is around, or find a field somewhere and set up some markers at zero, 50, 75, 100, 125, 150, 175, and 200 yards. Stand at the "zero" point and study them awhile. Then approach them from different angles and try to get a better *sense* of their distance from you and from each other.

Check your ability to judge distance on the course

Next time you're on the course, make an honest attempt to guess the shot yardage before relying on your caddie or a marker. Sensing the distance to the target is an art, and is as important as sensing the other components of the target picture. Developing that sense is therefore to be encouraged. You may want to play an entire round by attempting to sense the distance and then trusting your judgment, regardless of the result. In addition to learning a lot about your ability to sense the target, you'll enjoy the game all the more when you find that you were able to accurately gauge the distance.

The players of yesterday were masters of this art, and until the late 1950s and early 1960s, when Deane Beman and Jack Nicklaus popularized the measuring of distances between course landmarks, most players sensed the yardage without any help. Of course, it is very helpful to know the exact yardage. But don't select your club solely on that basis, while ignoring the wind, the lie, and the rest of the target picture.

Sensing the distance to your target

Now let's move on to the second component of the target picture.

2. The Terrain Around the Target

When the ball lands, it tends to act in a certain way based on the slope and hardness of the terrain surrounding the target. From your previous golfing experiences you know that, although the ball can sometimes take some unexpected hops, it generally bounces and rolls with the slope of the land. I find that having the opportunity to devise a run-up shot to the green and/or flag, if I so choose, over firm, sloping terrain covered with short grass, can make a course much more enjoyable to play. It's the way the game evolved over four-hundred-plus years, and it's why I've always loved the Old Course at St. Andrews, Scotland.

Being able to gauge the terrain around the target when putting is called "reading the green." It is an instinctual skill developed by practicing all types of putts on as many types of greens as you can.

CHECK YOUR AWARENESS OF THE TERRAIN

The next time you are out on the course, take a close look at the ground around your targets. Does it slope toward you or away from you? Is it hard or soft, dry or damp, fast or slow? What is the length and condition of the grass on the slopes? Can you run the ball or must you fly it and stop it quick? How can the terrain around the target help or hurt you?

ROLL BALLS TO SENSE THE TERRAIN

Go to the practice putting or chipping green and toss some balls underhand one at a time toward a hole—preferably one that's seventy or eighty feet away—*instinctively* allowing for the slope and speed of the green. Make the toss with a quiet mind and watch the motion of each ball until it stops, just being aware and observing what happens. How close are the balls to your target when they stop?

Now, instead of tossing one ball at a time, toss several all at once. Watch them track across the green until they come to rest, again keeping a quiet mind. The amount of feedback about the nature of the terrain increases with each ball, thus fueling your instincts.

Sensing the terrain by tracking balls across the green

Sense the terrain behind your target

When observing the terrain around the target, always be sure to take a look at the terrain *behind* your target, regardless of whether your target is the hole on the green or another spot elsewhere on the course.

Observing the terrain behind *the target*

Most golfers are only aware of the ground between themselves and the target, which is why most golf shots are left in that area, short of the target. (When you're playing in a foursome, do you ever notice that the percentage of iron shots hit to the green that stop short of the flag is always much larger than the percentage of those that finish past the flag?) Since most golfers only see the area short of and up to the target, they generally underclub themselves. This forces them to overswing, causing miss-hits which fall short of the target. Only their very best shots have a chance of getting there. What is your ratio of shots hit over the green to shots hit short? I'll bet it's very small, as is the case with most golfers.

When you take into account the terrain behind the target, you program your subconscious with a more comfortable sense of the target, one that's more centered rather than at the limits of your awareness. This greatly facilitates the selection of the right club (generally a stronger one) and the execution of a smoother swing, resulting in a shot that has a greater tendency to finish pin-high. A good rule for most amateurs to follow, when you cannot sense which club to use, is to take the longer club. This allows you to make a smoother, better-paced swing.

What's true for the fairway is also true for the putting green: always take a look at the ground behind the hole. Your awareness of the hole, and what you instinctively need to do to putt the ball into it, will thus become more comfortable and centered.

Observing the terrain behind *the target: the putting green*

FOLLOW THE BALL UNTIL IT STOPS ROLLING

Whenever you play a shot on the course, always follow the shot with your eyes until the ball stops rolling. You learn something about how a ball bounces and rolls on the terrain around the target every time you play a shot, and even

Watching the ball until it stops rolling

though you may have played it poorly, you are programming your subconscious with valuable information. Again, this applies to putting as well as every other kind of shot.

Now let's explore the third component of the target picture, the wind.

3. *The Wind*

The wind is the most underestimated part of the golf course, and one about which most amateurs seem to have little knowledge. It can easily affect your whole golfing psyche before you ever swing. After the ball leaves the clubface, the wind is the only thing affecting its flight until it hits the ground (provided there are no trees in the way). How does the wind affect you mentally? Do you tense up when it's blowing in your face? Do your grip pressure and confidence level tend to vary according to whether the wind is directly in your face or directly behind you? Do you hit the ball high, where the wind can have a greater effect on the ball flight path? Do you have a feel for striking a low, or "knock-down" shot?

How good is your sense of direction? How hard does the wind blow at your club? From which direction does the prevailing wind come? More importantly, do you recognize any patterns the wind may have throughout the day, the season, or the year? Once, when I was playing the Old Course at St. Andrews, my caddie pulled a little notebook from his pocket and charted the wind for the day. He had done so every day for years and had built up quite a bit of instinctive knowledge about the wind there. Needless to say, he was a great caddie.

So, how do we develop an instinct for the wind? Try the following exercises.

Sense the wind while walking with a friend

Go for a long walk, say five miles on a semi-winding trail, with a friend, spouse, or fellow golfer, in an area where the wind blows. Just obey this one rule: always keep your partner between you and the direction the wind is coming from. This exercise requires your total attention—if you carry on a conversation, you will not benefit from it. *You must stay aware of the wind the whole time.* If you do, you will be amazed. Not only will you begin to develop an instinct for the speed and direction of the wind; you will also begin to feel you can *anticipate* changes in the wind. You'll notice that the wind truly has a life of its own.

An exercise in sensing the wind

Learn to sense direction at your course

Find out which way is due north at your golf course or club. Then, teach yourself to locate north anywhere on the course at any time of the day.

Observe the wind patterns where you normally play

Next time you're on the course, make a quick note on the scorecard of the date and tee-off time, and the direction and speed of the wind. If, while playing, you notice any significant changes in the wind, jot that down too. Try to get the club to install a weathervane or a flag in a prominent place near the first tee. The wind is a very important part of the golf course. You don't want to become mechanical about the wind, just aware of its force, direction, and patterns or routines.

The wind is an important part of the golf course

WATCH HOW THE WIND AFFECTS THE BALL FLIGHT PATH

The next time a strong wind blows, go to the practice tee and have some fun. Strike shots with your normal swing and watch carefully how the wind affects the ball's flight. Remember, just use your normal swing and keep a very quiet mind. And if the wind is blowing strongly from left to right, don't hit full shots for longer than fifteen or twenty minutes.

No doubt about it, the wind definitely affects the flight of the golf ball. Granted, a well-struck shot can be substantially less affected than an off-center hit. But in either case, the wind will still have some effect.

The black line is your ball flight path. The white line is the direction of your swing path through the ball.

Now, let's move on to the fourth component of the target picture, the lie.

4. The Lie

How many times have you hit a shot and not understood why the ball flew like it did? Chances are the lie had something to do with it. One of the great things about the game of golf is that no two lies are exactly the same!

Do you always play the ball as it lies? Do you think negatively, and subconsciously prepare yourself for a negative result when you come upon your ball and find the lie less than perfect? Or when you find your ball in a bunker, or in the trees? Does this affect your demeanor? When the ball is sitting down in the grass does your grip pressure increase because you feel you have to "hit" the ball harder? Do you worry about hitting it "fat" or "skulling" it off hardpan? Do you notice how the ball's flight is affected when grass gets between the clubface and the ball or when you're playing off wet grass?

Do you notice how the clubface can get twisted in your hands when you're swinging through long grass? Are you aware of your limitations in club selection and trajectory from lies in medium to long grass, and do you have the patience to just knock the ball straight back to the fairway when you have to? Do you notice how far your ball ends up from the ball mark when it lands on the green? How about on the fairway?

Pulling the ball from long grass

WATCH HOW THE LIE AFFECTS THE FLIGHT
OF THE GOLF BALL

When you're on the practice tee and around the practice green, practice from all kinds of lies, including different sand shots. Don't try to do anything different, just observe how various lies affect the ball flight path when you make your normal swing. Again, be sure to watch the complete flight of the ball, including how it lands and the amount of bounce and roll.

Fairway   In a divot

First cut of rough   Firm sand

A "flier"   Hardpan

Observe what happens when you strike a shot from a "flying" lie. A "flier" is a lie, generally in the medium-length rough, that allows grass to get between the ball and club-face at impact. This decreases the normal amount of backspin on the ball, causing it to fly lower and farther, with more roll when it lands.

Strike shots from long, medium and short grass with the ball sitting up and sitting down. Strike shots off hardpan and from divot holes. Be sure to practice these shots with various clubs. Again, just make your normal swing and watch what happens.

PLAY THE BALL AS IT LIES

I strongly recommend that every golfer live by the rule, "play the ball as it lies." If the embedded ball rule is in effect through the green and your ball is plugged, then by all means, take a drop. But remember: it is only from playing out of all kinds of lies that you will acquire the instinctive knowledge necessary to handle a difficult lie. And always watch the flight of the ball and keep watching until it stops, an activity that programs your subconscious with valuable information.

Incidentally, I find that golf is much more rewarding when you succeed in making a good shot from a difficult situation rather than making a good shot after you've improved your lie in the fairway. In fact, I feel more pressure on the latter shot because, having improved my lie, I'm now *supposed* to make a good shot. That's why I'm bothered by the frequent usage of winter rules. Playing it as it lies is the backbone of golf!

Now we investigate the fifth component of the target picture, the "slope of the stance."

5. *The Slope of the Stance*

When I speak of different slopes of the stance, I'm referring to uphill and downhill stances, and sidehill stances where the ball is either higher or lower than your feet. In my opinion, the effect of the slope of the stance on the ball flight path is also vastly underestimated by most amateur golfers. Anyone who has ever pulled a shot way left from an uphill lie or sliced one when the ball was lower than their feet can attest to this. Are you familiar with the tendencies of the ball flight from these various stances?

OBSERVE HOW THE SLOPE OF THE STANCE AFFECTS THE BALL FLIGHT PATH

You'll have to go out on the course by yourself for this exercise, when nobody else is around and you can play three or four balls. Find a good uphill lie and hit a few shots with a wedge or 9-iron, a few with a middle iron like the 6, and a few with a long iron such as the 3. Don't make any adjustments in your aim or swing, but do adjust your setup to make your shoulders as parallel to the slope as you can. Again, keep a quiet mind and just observe the effects of the uphill stance on the ball flight path. Then do the same from a downhill stance. Next, locate a sidehill stance with the ball higher than the feet and do the same exercise. Do it again with the ball lower than the feet. In just a very short time you will gain an instinctive feel for the various slopes of the stance. The more you practice this exercise, the more you will be programming your subconscious with excellent information.

Uphill slope

Downhill slope

Sidehill—ball above feet

Sidehill—ball below feet

6. The Ball Flight Path

The first goal of this chapter was to get you on the road to becoming instinctively aware of the first five components of the target picture, which we have just examined. By gaining an instinctive knowledge of each component, you will be able to immediately sense the sixth and final component of the target picture, the ball flight path. That is the second goal of this chapter.

The black line is your ball flight path. The white line is the direction of your swing path through the ball.

To illustrate this point, let's take an example:

VISUALIZING THE BALL FLIGHT PATH—EXAMPLE I

We've chosen our target to be the hole, 150 yards away, in the middle of a large, flat green. A steady breeze is blowing from left to right, you have a clean lie in the fairway, the ball lies slightly lower than your feet, and the natural shape of your shots is fairly straight. From doing the exercises in this chapter, and from your previous golfing experiences, you will be able to instinctively judge the combined effects of the wind and the slope of the stance on the shot, and visualize your intended ball flight path.

First we'll examine the effect of the wind. As you stand behind the ball observing the target picture, you can sense

Wind

Sensing the combined effects of the wind and the slope of the stance on the ball flight path of the shot

how the ball flight path may have to start out more to the left than it otherwise would, because you know instinctively that the left-to-right wind will bring the ball back to the right. Sense how much farther left than normal the ball flight path may have to start. Don't try to do this scientifically with a formula for just how many feet to the left the ball must start based on the estimated wind velocity, etc., etc. You want to try to sense the effect *instinctively*—literally feel it in your gut; sense the effect the wind will have on the ball as it flies to the target; sense how much farther left the ball flight path may have to begin to accommodate the effect of the wind. Let's say you sense the wind will have an effect on your flight path equal to the amount A as shown in the photograph on page 57.

Now do the same thing as you did with the wind to try to sense the effect the slope of the stance will have on the ball flight path. As you stand behind the shot, sense how much farther left than normal the ball flight path may have to begin in order to accommodate the effect of the slope of the stance. Let's say you sense that the ball below the feet will have an effect on the ball flight path equal to the amount B as shown on page 57.

Now you want to get an instinctive sense of the combined effect of these two components of the target picture, the wind *and* the slope of the stance, on the ball flight path. Inasmuch as the effects of the components of the target picture are cumulative, you will probably visualize or sense that the combined effect of both components on the ball flight path will be close to the sum of the two individual effects.

So you may sense that your ball flight path will look like path C in the following photograph.

Sensing the combined effects of a left-to-right wind and the ball below your feet on the ball flight path of the shot

Next, with this visualization serving as a guide, you may instinctively select your club, perhaps choosing a 6-iron. The idea here is that by sensing the target picture, including visualizing the ball flight path, you will have a much more instinctive idea of which club to use and how your swing should feel. Let's look at another example.

VISUALIZING THE BALL FLIGHT PATH—EXAMPLE 2

You're on the tee of a slight dogleg left, 400-yard par 4 with a pretty wide fairway. You've got a driver in your hand. There's a good solid breeze blowing from right to left. And the pin is cut on the back left of the green, so the best approach is from somewhere on the right side of the fairway.

Sensing the combined effects of a right-to-left wind and an intentional fade on the ball flight path of the shot

First, you sense the effect the wind may have. Then you sense how, in this case, an intentional fade will offset rather than add to the effect of the wind. (We will talk about how to intentionally curve the ball in Chapter 8).

Again, I must say that you don't want to get scientific about the extent to which the first five components of the target picture will affect the ball flight path. How you adjust your setup to account for the effect of these target picture components will be done just as instinctively as you sensed them. As you gain more and more experience instinctively sensing different combinations of target picture components and then letting your swing react to each of those target pictures, you will become more adept at sensing the magnitude of those combined effects on the flight of the golf ball.

Whether the natural shape of your shots is normally left to right, straight, or right to left doesn't matter when it comes to instinctively sensing the ball flight path. If your "natural" ball flight path is a fade or a draw, that means you have an instinctive way of curving the ball on most shots. When you sense the effects of the different components of the target picture on the flight path your ball will take, you will instinctively take into account your natural tendencies. For example, if you are aware of how much you normally fade a 5-iron from a flat lie in the fairway with no wind, then you will instinctively be able to sense the offsetting effect that a right-to-left wind, or a lie with the ball above your feet, will have. You will then instinctively sense your proper ball flight path based on all this information.

Don't worry if, as you stand behind the ball observing the target picture, you do not see a brightly illuminated ball flight path spread before you in the sky. All you are looking for is a sense or a feel for the path the ball will take. Once you gain enough instinctive knowledge of the target picture components and their effect on the ball flight path, and combine that with a quiet mind, you just may start to spontaneously visualize those streamers in the sky!

By sensing the intended ball flight path of your shot, you'll discover that you're able to instinctively feel the setup and swing motion necessary to propel the ball to your target.

So, now you have a feeling of what to observe before the shot. You look at your target and the terrain around it, sense the effects that the wind, the lie, and the slope of the stance will have on the shot, and sense the path the ball will take to your target. That's it! The more you use the above exercises to develop an instinct for sensing the effects the first five components of the target picture will have on the flight of the ball, the easier it gets to visualize your intended ball flight path on each individual shot. Before long, you'll realize that, just by observing the shot from behind the ball, the ball flight path will *automatically be induced* in your senses.

Next, you'll discover how to feel your swing as a reaction to the target.

CHAPTER 5

Feeling Your Swing as a Reaction to the Target

In the previous chapter you became aware of, and began to enhance, your instinctive sense for those things taking place *outside* of you—the components of the target picture. In this chapter you will focus on experiencing the feel of the swing motion that will propel the ball to your target along your intended ball flight path.

When you learn to drive a car on a highway, you're taught to set your sights on a point a good distance down the road. That way, your immediate driving actions prior to reaching that point get taken care of more or less subconsciously. You sense the "picture" down the road and react naturally to it. In other words, you are driving instinctively. Similarly, you are going to learn to feel yourself swinging a club as an instinctive reaction to the target.

In this chapter I am not going to tell you specifically in what position or place to put the club or clubhead, or how or in what exact position any part of your body should be. That entails mechanical thoughts. Instead, I am going to give you exercises designed to let you become aware of what it is you're actually doing.

A famous philosopher named Krishnamurti once said, "The answer to a problem always lies within the problem." So, first you must become aware of the problem; that is, you must become aware of what it is you are doing wrong. If you just try to do what others tell you, without investigating and becoming aware of what it is you are actually doing, then you will never truly become aware of what it is you are actually doing *wrong*.

So, instead of trying to do what someone else says you should do, you are just going to become aware of what it is you are actually doing. In developing that awareness, you will learn to sense what you are doing wrong, and beneficial changes will occur instinctively and spontaneously. Moreover, such changes will take place instantaneously, if only you observe, feel, and be aware.

Swinging with Target Awareness

The six exercises in this chapter are designed to give you the very basic idea of what it means to swing the club with target awareness. The first exercise teaches you to focus your awareness on what you're feeling inside when you simulate a golf swing in slow motion. The second exercise teaches you to hold a sense of where the target is even though you're not looking at it. The following four exercises *unite* those swing feelings with your awareness of the target.

In these exercises, you are going to simplify your target picture by temporarily disregarding the following four components: the terrain around the target, the wind, the lie, and the slope of the stance. The only components of the target picture you are going to work with here are the target and the ball flight path.

To best perform the following exercises, it is recommended that you first read through this whole chapter, including all the exercises, to get a feel of what you're going to be doing. It is further recommended that you then find a secluded spot outdoors, such as your backyard, to perform them.

Also, to enhance your awareness and feel during these exercises, and whenever you have a golf club in your hands:

Pay attention to your grip pressure. Be sure it is light enough so you can begin to feel the pace and position of the club-head during the swing. Strive to keep your grip pressure constant during the swing. Notice any tendency you may have to increase it, especially during the takeaway, at the beginning of the downswing, and just before impact.

Exercise 1.

Sensing the swing in slow motion, with eyes closed, without a target and without a club

First, stand in the address position for a 5-iron shot, but without a club or a ball. Let your hands come together and make their normal grip. Close your eyes and, without any target in mind, take a full swing, but in slow motion. Repeat the swing several times, always in slow motion. Do not swing back and forth like a pendulum; instead, make each swing individually, stopping after the follow-through is complete, and then start again from the address position.

As you swing the club, be aware of what your hands are doing. How are they moving? Are they rotating? Are your palms facing in a certain direction as they rotate? Is there tension in your hands?

Don't try or think that you must change anything you're doing; that's not why you're here. Just keep your eyes closed and observe or be cognizant of your feelings at every moment. The key is just to be aware and to experience each new feeling or sensation. Stay in the present and keep sensing what you're doing, and don't let your mind wander.

After doing this, say, six or seven times, become aware of what your arms are doing. How are they turning? In what direction are they swinging? Do you feel tension in them? Next, do the same with your shoulders, then your mid-section. Feel what your chest and back are doing, which way they're pointing, and when. Then your hips, followed by your knees and feet. Do a few swings each time. Just stay aware of what is happening.

Feeling your body move as you swing in slow motion

Exercise 2.

Sensing the target

Now, pick a target. Since you are outdoors, any flagstick, tree, or fence post will do. As you did in the section on sensing the target in Chapter 4, take a good look at your target and take a moment to notice its shadows and highlights, lines, and colors. Sense the distance to your target. Try not to think in terms of feet or yards for now, but rather just get a sense of "farness" or "closeness" compared to the distances of other objects.

Then, assume your address position, without a ball or club, as if you were going to play a shot to that target. Rotate your head to the left until you are looking at the target. Don't lift your head when you do this. Then close your eyes and rotate your head back to where the ball would be. From this position, raise your left arm (if you play right-handed), and point to the exact location of your target. Then open your eyes, observe where you were pointing, and see how accurate you were.

You may be slightly off, or you may be right on the mark. At any rate, do this about ten times. Before long you will get quite good at it. You are beginning to gain a sense of precisely where the target is, even though you are not looking at it.

Sensing the location of the target from address without a club

Exercise 3.

Sensing the swing in slow motion with eyes closed, with a target but without a club

You are going to repeat Exercise 1, but this time with an awareness of your target in mind. Assume your address position, without a ball or a club, as if you were going to play a shot to your target. Sense the location of your target, as you learned to do in Exercise 2, and sense the flight path a ball would take to it. Close your eyes and make your individual, slow-motion swings with the target sense in your mind. Do not open your eyes to see where your target is; instead, trust that you are sensing its location accurately. If you have difficulty sensing the location of your target, repeat Exercise 2.

Feel all the parts of your body as they *relate* to the direction and distance of the target when you swing, and as they *react* to the direction and distance of the target. You don't have a club or ball, you are just relating the motions of your body to the target sense in your mind. Feel yourself in a normal address position, aligned in such a way that you will swing away from and then back toward the target you are sensing.

Feel the movements of your hands and arms as you did in Exercise 1, but now feel these movements *as they relate to the target*. Feel yourself turn back far enough to develop the power needed to propel the ball to the target, no more and no less. Feel the position of your hands with respect to the target as you move through the entire swing motion. Notice the same feelings with respect to the target of your shoulders, back, hips, legs, and feet. Feel yourself turn away from the target and then turn through toward it.

With respect to the target, where is your back positioned at the top of the backswing? Does it face the target? Where is your chest positioned at the finish of the swing? Does it face the target? Isn't keeping the eyes closed a great way to sense what you're feeling inside?

Again, don't feel that you must try to change anything you are doing; the important thing is just to feel the effect your mind's target sense has on how you swing. Do this exercise a number of times until the sensations of the swing

Feeling your body react to the location of the target as you swing in slow motion

motion with respect to the target become familiar. You are beginning to learn how to play golf with target awareness.

Exercise 4.

Sensing the swing in slow motion with eyes closed,
with a target, with a club, but without a ball

Next, grasp a 5-iron. Repeat Exercise 3. Again, sense the location of your target and the flight path your ball will take to the target. Feel yourself comfortably set up to the target picture, and hold that target sense in your mind as you move the club. Keep your eyes closed and make your individual swings in slow motion.

Feel the relationship between the way you set your hands on the club and the direction in which the clubface is pointing. Feel how the position of your clubface changes in relation to the target as you move through the entire swing motion. Feel how the different parts of your body—the hands, arms, shoulders, trunk, hips, legs, and feet—react to the location of your target. Sense how big your backswing must be to send the ball the entire distance to the target. Feel the weight of the club. Do this a number of times until the sensations of the motion of your body and the club *with respect to the target* become familiar.

Be sure to keep your grip light, with no tension in your forearms and shoulders.

As in the other exercises, don't be concerned with where any part of you or the club *should be*. Since it is more important to know where the club *is* rather than where it *should be*, just stay aware, keeping your mind as quiet as you can.

Sensing the location of the target from address while holding a club

Feeling your body and the club react to the location of the target as you swing in slow motion

Exercise 5.

Sensing the swing with eyes closed, with a target, with a club, but without a ball

Now, repeat Exercise 4, this time swinging the club normally and not in slow motion. Again, keep your eyes closed and sense the location of your target and your ball flight path to the target.

You want to feel all the same things you felt in the preceding exercises. Feel the path and pace of the swinging club in relation to the target. Feel how the position of the clubface changes with respect to the target as you move through the entire swing motion. Feel your body turning directly away from the target and then turning back toward the target. Just as before, feel the hands, arms, shoulders, back, chest, hips, legs, and feet; feel what each is doing with respect to the target.

Be sure to pay attention to your grip pressure, keeping it constant and light enough to feel the swinging clubhead.

Notice how, when you're reacting to the target instead of the ball, you feel much more motion, acceleration, and follow-through in the post-impact phase of your swing.

To make sure you are getting a real "swinging" sensation here, you may want to imagine you are swinging a bucket of water. This forces you to make a correct swinging motion backward *and* forward to prevent the water from falling out of the bucket. The lighter your grip, the better, but be careful not to let your hands loosen too much and change position on, or let go of, the club. Feel the swinging force of the club, like the weight of the water in the bucket, throughout the *entire* swing, and with respect to the target. Or, instead of a bucket, think about the motion of a playground swing or a pendulum. I personally like the bucket-of-water image, but use whatever works.

Do this as long as it takes to become familiar with the sensations of the swinging motion of your body and the club *with respect to your awareness of the target.* Then do it a little longer.

EXERCISE 6.

Sensing the swing with eyes open, with a target and a club but without a ball

Repeat Exercise 5, except with your eyes open. This is going to make it more difficult to internalize the feel of the swing with respect to the target, so if you ever need to regain your target sense when you swing, repeat the exercise with your eyes closed.

As you make your swings, be sure to feel the same things you were feeling in Exercise 5. Sense the target and the ball flight path to the target. Just as before, feel what each part of your body is doing with respect to the target. Feel the path of the swinging clubhead and what your hands and clubface are doing with respect to the target. Feel your body turning directly away from the target and then turning back toward the target.

Be sure you feel a lightness in the arms and shoulders, and keep a light, constant grip pressure so you can feel the path and pace of the swinging clubhead in relation to the target. Clip the grass lightly as you swing through.

Notice how, when you're reacting to the target instead of the ball, you feel much more motion, acceleration, and follow-through in the post-impact phase of your swing. Be sure to feel the pace of your swing in the same way you did in Exercise 5.

Remember, you are not "trying" to do anything here, you're just staying aware of how your body and club feel as your swing reacts to the target.

By now you will have been able to make a pretty strong connection between the target and the swinging motion of your body and the club. This is the *swing* instinct, and it is something you want to utilize when your eyes are open and you're using a ball. As you learned in Chapter 2, that is where the difficulty lies, for it is ever so easy to lose your focus on the target and revert back to the ball, thus becoming *ball bound* instead of *target bound*.

Upon completing these exercises, you will have acquired a lot of instinctive knowledge about the feel of your swing as a reaction to the target. At the end of the previous chapter, you learned that, as you gained experience sensing the first five components of the target picture, the sixth component, the ball flight path, was automatically induced in your senses. Likewise, as you continue to sense the ball flight path to your target, the swing feel necessary to react to that target becomes automatically induced, and this will enable you to become more instinctive about choosing the correct club.

In these exercises a simplified target picture was used with just the target and the ball flight path to the target. In Chapter 4 you observed that, because of the effects of the terrain around the target, as well as the wind, the lie, and the slope of the stance, the initial direction of your intended ball flight path is often to the right or left of a line straight from the ball to your target. Whenever you set up to a

The black line is your ball flight path. The white line is the direction of your swing path through the ball.

shot, you want to feel that you are set up so that your swing will start the ball in the *initial* direction of your intended ball flight path. This is examined in more detail in Chapter 7, under the heading "Addressing the Shot with Target Awareness."

Next, you will find out how, by learning to maintain your target awareness throughout the entire swing, you can take the knowledge you have learned thus far and use it to trust yourself to instinctively react to the target picture when you play.

CHAPTER 6

Maintaining Your Awareness of the Target Throughout the Entire Swing

One of the secrets to playing golf with target awareness is to keep your awareness focused on the target picture throughout the entire shot. If you only keep it for part of the swing, you set yourself up for reverting back to the ball and once again becoming ball bound, which can cause inconsistent shots and frustration. So far in the exercises you have been programming your subconscious to react to your awareness of the target picture. But that cannot happen if you lose your sense of that target picture just before or during the swing. You cannot trust your subconscious to react to something that's not there.

Trust Your Subconscious

Trust, that's the magic word. Whenever you allow yourself to act instinctively, which means without thought or conscious act, you are implying a trust in yourself, a trust that your instincts will carry the day and result in a beneficial outcome to whatever you are doing. Trust is not easy to develop, because it involves taking a risk. So, if you can improve your target focus during the swing, you can become better able to trust your subconscious to perform correctly. The upcoming exercises are designed to do just that.

As you have already noticed, closing your eyes is an excellent learning aid to sensing what you are feeling inside when you perform an action. Some of these exercises again take advantage of that wonderful learning technique and doorway to the inner self.

EXERCISE 1.

Sensing the location of the target after turning with eyes closed

As in previous exercises, pick out a target and observe it carefully, noting any distinguishing characteristics. Then close your eyes and slowly spin a couple of times. Or, better still, have a friend spin you, just like when you used to play pin-the-tail-on-the-donkey. Now, without opening your eyes, point to your target. This is similar to Exercise 2 in Chapter 5, except now you are moving around a lot more and making it more difficult to keep a sense of exactly where the target is. And yet, if you do this exercise regularly, you will develop a finely tuned instinctive awareness of exactly where your target is, regardless of how your body may be moving or where your eyes may be looking.

Turn around with your eyes closed and still maintain your sense of the location of the target

In his book *Shape Your Swing the Modern Way*, Byron Nelson says, "Don't think of hitting at the ball, rather think of contact as being from the ball on through. You should actually feel the clubhead being thrown at the target." Nelson cautions, however, "Don't try to make this happen, rather program the image in your mind beforehand and then just let it happen."

The next four exercises are designed to help you maintain a sense of the target throughout the entire swing, and to help you understand how maintaining a target sense programs you to swing "from the ball on through."

The post-impact part of the swing: "from the ball on through"

Exercise 2.

Throwing clubs at the target

I learned about this exercise a few years ago at the *Golf in the Kingdom* seminars, and I think it is one of the best for maintaining your target focus. Get some old clubs that you no longer use. Take maybe ten of them to your yard, a field, or anywhere you have a good bit of room. Pick a spot and mark it with a handkerchief, a cushion—anything that can be used as a target. Then, go to a spot about thirty yards away.

This exercise is divided into three parts.

Part 1. Take a club, and set up like you are going to swing toward your target. Then rotate your head and let your eyes follow a straight line from your imaginary ball position to the target. Be careful not to lift your head while rotating it. *With your eyes fixed on the target*, swing the club back and then through, letting go of it at just the right time so it flies through the air toward the target. In other words, throw the club at the target while you are swinging the club as you would for a normal golf shot, except you are looking at the target while you swing. Feel the proper length of backswing you need to throw the club the exact distance to the target, no more and no less. This is not as easy as it looks, but it's a great exercise. With a little practice, you can get quite good at it. Throw all your clubs, then repeat the exercise several times.

Don't worry about how high you throw the clubs. And there's no need to power them hard at the target. Just keep

your grip light and send the clubs softly sailing to the target. This is an excellent exercise that really promotes your
target focus while you swing. If you get proficient at thirty
yards you may want to increase the distance to the target to

Part 1: Throwing a club while looking at the target

forty or fifty yards. Just remember, the key is not how far
you can throw the clubs, but how accurately.

Part 2. Repeat Part 1, but after rotating your head to the
target, rotate it back to your imaginary ball position and then
throw the club. Instead of looking at the target as you throw,
you'll be trusting your target sense. Again, throw all the clubs
a number of times until you can hit the target consistently.

Part 2: Throwing a club while looking at the ball position

Part 3. Repeat Part 2, but close your eyes before you swing the club and don't open them until the club has left your hands. Again, you will be trusting your target sense for this part of the exercise. In a relatively short time you will enhance your target sense and become quite accurate. Stay with this exercise until you do. Along with heightening your awareness of the target throughout the entire swing, this exercise gives you an excellent sense of the proper swing feel needed to react to the target.

EXERCISE 3.
Tuning in to the ball flight path

This is an exercise I learned from Bob Toski many years ago, and it will help you stay attuned to your intended ball flight path. You'll need a thin stick about three feet long or a club-shaft with the head broken off. Pick a target and stick the shaft in the ground just ahead of your swing path in the direction of, and at the same initial angle of trajectory as, your intended ball flight path. This exercise enables you to better sense before and during the swing the relationship between your body, your intended swing path and clubface position through the ball, and your ball flight path. Do this exercise with different clubs, ranging from the wedge to the long irons. Observe how the initial trajectory changes with

Tuning in to the ball flight path, part 1

each one and adjust the angle of the club shaft in the ground accordingly.

The second part of this exercise is a variation of a drill imparted to me by Fred Shoemaker. Begin this exercise with a pitching wedge, adjusting the angle of the shaft in the ground for the normally steeper trajectory of that club. Next, set up to a ball with your body and club in the position they would be at *impact* rather than at address. Then, sense your target and, without any backswing, push-swing through with the hands and arms, propelling the ball toward the target. Repeat this exercise until you have a feel for sustaining an awareness of the target through your body and club for the entire follow-through. Then switch to the sand wedge and repeat. This exercise is good because it can be especially dif-

Tuning in to the ball flight path, part 2

ficult to sustain your target focus and overcome the *hit* impulse with the shorter clubs and shorter "part" swings.

Exercise 4.
Use a ribbon to promote the proper swing path and alignment

Here's another exercise I learned from Toski, one that will really help you feel, from the address position, a proper swing path. Go to the range and choose a target. Starting from about three feet behind the ball, tack a ten-yard strip of ribbon in the direction you wish to swing. Tee up a ball in the middle of the ribbon. Set your clubface behind the ball, aiming down the ribbon, and align your body to the ribbon. Rotate your head toward the target without lifting it, and let your eyes track down the ribbon. Then rotate your head back all the way to the end of the ribbon behind the ball. Rotate your head forward again until you can see the ball, and then swing. This exercise lets you sense the direction of your target, promotes a proper swing path, gives you an excellent sense of the necessary alignment of your body and club at address to accommodate that swing path, and enhances your awareness of the position of your hands and clubface during the swing.

Using a ribbon to sense the proper direction of your swing path at address

EXERCISE 5.

Listening to the shaft swing through the air

Grasp a club with a normal grip on the opposite end of the shaft, near the clubhead. With a target in mind, make a swing and listen for the "whoosh" sound the shaft makes as it swings through the air. Notice the location of the sound. It should come in the post-impact phase of your swing. This is a good exercise to do on the course when you want to regain your feel for the *swing* instinct.

The following three exercises continue to deal with over-coming the *hit* instinct and replacing it with a free-flowing *swing* instinct through target awareness.

EXERCISE 6.

Playing with the feel of a practice swing

Select a 7-iron for this exercise. Pick out a target on the range as far away as you normally strike that club. As you've done in previous exercises, sense the location of your target and hold that sense in your mind. Next, make six practice swings to your target. However, before you make these swings ask yourself, "If I could have my choice of any swing in the world, what kind of a feel would it have?" This is your chance to give yourself a flowing rhythm and a silky smooth pace. Close your eyes if you like, lighten your grip pressure if nec-essary, and feel the most fluid, "oily" swing you can. Then make your practice swings with *that* feel. Be sure to keep your grip pressure the same during the entire swing. Then step up to a shot with a ball and make the same target-aware practice swing, letting the ball get in the way of your swing to the target. *Do not concern yourself with where the ball goes.*

After this swing, make six more practice swings exactly as before; then one more shot with a ball. Repeat several times.

The purpose of this drill is to learn to strike the ball with the feel of a target-oriented practice swing and to rid yourself of any tendency to try to "hit" the ball. Doing this drill for a while will help eliminate any *hit* impulse you may have. The key is to swing to the target on the shots with the ball, in the exact same way you did with your practice swings, without any concern for what happens to the ball.

In learning this drill, you'll realize that with a proper setup, *the ball merely gets in the way of the club being swung to the target.* Before long, you'll find your shots flying farther and straighter, with less effort, than ever before.

Exercise 7.
Removing a ball from the path of a swinging club

If you have difficulty repeating the smooth pace of a practice swing when you are over the ball, this exercise may help. It was popularized by the well-known instructor Harvey Penick and, like the previous exercise, helps to cure a golfer's preoccupation with the ball. You'll need the aid of a friend. Thumbtack a couple of yards of thin string to each of five or six old balls. As you tee up each ball, your friend should hold the end of the line, ready to yank the ball off the tee before impact, but without telling you when he or she is going to do it. You will begin not to think about the ball because you won't know if it will still be on the tee when the clubhead comes through. This will enable you to make that nice silky practice swing when you are over the ball.

Removing a ball from the path of a swinging club—long shots

EXERCISE 8.

Inserting a ball in the path of a swinging club—short shots

You can do this entire exercise on the putting green or at home on a rug, but in either case you'll need a friend to help you. I learned the first part of this exercise at the *Golf in the Kingdom* seminars.

Take a putter and set up to a putt, but without a ball or a target. Begin swinging the putter back and forth with a pendulum motion, striving for a smooth stroke. Ask yourself a question similar to the one you asked in Exercise 6: "If I could have my choice of any putting stroke in the world, what kind of a feel would the stroke have?" Then swing the putter back and forth with *that* feel.

Ask your friend to randomly put a ball down in the path of the putterhead while your putter is somewhere in the backswing. Have he or she do this repeatedly, yet randomly enough so you won't know when to expect it. The key here is to keep swinging with the same smooth feel when a ball is introduced to the swing that you have without the ball. Be aware of any added tension you may feel in your hands when the ball appears. Such tension is a product of the *hit* impulse.

Now have your friend put a ball down and then, just as you're about to hit it, quickly snatch it away. Do you feel yourself jerk or change rhythm when the ball disappears? That reaction is also a product of the *hit* impulse.

Do this drill for a while until you are sure you have overcome your *hit* impulse and have developed a *swing* instinct.

Then do the second part of this exercise: Find a hole on the green, or use a putting cup on your rug, and stroke putts of varying lengths. Sense the target, and use the same smooth feel of the *swing* instinct you just developed. You might try this with a few chip shots as well.

Inserting a ball in the path of a swinging club—short shots

Exercise 9.

Sensing where the ball has gone with your eyes closed

This is one of the most challenging, yet rewarding, exercises I know. It is performed on the putting green and the range. The assistance of a friend is recommended but not absolutely necessary.

Find a straight putt about fifteen feet long and set up to the putt. Station your friend behind the shot looking down the line of the putt toward the hole.

Sense the target, then close your eyes and strike the putt. Keep your eyes closed until the ball has stopped rolling. Before you open them, announce to your friend where you think the ball has finished (left, right, or straight; short, long, or in the hole), based on what you felt from swinging the putter and contacting the ball. Your friend should tell you where the ball actually went.

If you're alone, announce to yourself what you sensed the results of the putt were and then, after giving the putt time to stop rolling, open your eyes, and compare what really happened to what you felt.

Though difficult, this is a great exercise for developing "feel," or "touch."

Stick with it, even if it takes a long time to be able to tell what you did with your eyes closed. You'll be able to feel center and off-center hits, the direction your hands and the putter blade are facing, and the speed of the clubhead as it moves through the ball. Try some chip shots and, if you're feeling adventurous, go to the range and try some longer shots as well.

*Sensing
where the
ball has
gone with
your eyes
closed*

By now you should be developing a feel for swinging the club, both for short and long shots, with target awareness. In many of these exercises you even got to strike some shots, although within the framework of the individual exercise. In the next chapter, you will discover how to solidify what you've learned by creating a shot routine; then, in Chapter 8, you put it all together and start playing golf with target awareness.

CHAPTER 7

Creating Your Own Shot Routine

You have observed and perhaps even experienced how sensing the target picture can induce the proper swing feel needed to react to that picture. You have also begun to learn how to maintain a sense of the target picture throughout your entire swing. Now you've come to the part that will fully integrate what you've learned—the creation of the shot routine.

You may have heard this referred to as the *pre*-shot routine, and although it's only a matter of nomenclature, I don't believe the use of a routine in playing a golf shot is limited to just those movements *before* you swing. Moreover, I think making any note of an interruption, or a division, between pre-swing and swing is adverse to the unimpeded flow of motion and target sense so necessary from the waggle through the forward press and beyond to the finish of the swing.

The shot routine provides a consistent method of approaching and executing a golf shot. It is composed of a systematic series of movements and sensory feelings blended together through practice. The shot routine gives you a way to automatically execute your shots, especially under pressure. It lets you function on "auto pilot," so to speak, and deal with different golfing situations in a similar fashion. It places you in a sort of mental cocoon that shields you from the import of the moment and lets you pull the trigger. If you look at the golf games of good players, you'll find most all of them have a shot routine that is consistent and reliable.

The shot routine gives you the opportunity to gather your attention and focus on sensing the target picture and the proper swing feel necessary to react to the target picture.

It serves to quiet your mind, giving you the best opportunity to maintain your awareness of the target picture throughout the entire swing, thus enabling you to trust your swing to instinctively react to the target.

A well-conceived shot routine will speed up your play.

A correct shot routine encourages you to be target-oriented from the initial inspection of the circumstances and conditions surrounding a shot through the execution and the moments following the shot. By keeping you focused on the target picture, the shot routine serves to prevent you from having your focus revert back to the ball. A correct shot routine also keeps you constantly in motion, previewing the rhythm and feel of the shot and preventing tension from setting in and hindering the use of your golfing muscles. This combination of a steady target awareness and a continual rhythm of motion gives you the ability to execute your shots confidently and decisively.

Watch a top player like Tom Watson as he goes through his shot routine and executes his swing. Sense how his movements express his awareness of the target picture and preview the rhythm of his upcoming swing. Observe how that motion confidently takes him toward a decisive execution of his shot.

In short, the shot routine lets you visualize the shot and then trust yourself to execute that visualization.

A lot of amateurs are unaware of the benefits of a shot routine and therefore don't make the effort to create one for themselves. They either don't know how to do so, or they figure that a shot routine won't help them. In reality, the shot routine will solidify your game, free you between shots to enjoy your companions and surroundings, and help you stay cool when the heat is on. And make no mistake—all golfers, from the touring pro to the 20-handicapper playing a $1 Nassau with friends, feel the pressure in golf and want to do their best, especially on those pressure shots. So give yourself a consistent shot routine; the effort will be well worth it.

Please note that in the following discussion of the components of the shot routine, you need only be concerned with sensing the target picture, sensing the proper swing feel necessary to react to the target, and maintaining an awareness of the target throughout the entire swing. Do not be concerned here with the mechanics of the setup, such as weight distribution and posture, or the mechanics of any other component of the golf swing. Those are to be worked out on the practice tee and are discussed in Part III, "Practicing Golf."

Components of the Shot Routine

First, you'll examine in order the various parts of the shot routine. Then you'll put the parts together and discover how they blend into one continuous, flowing motion from beginning to end. Then you'll examine two other components— the imaginary shot and the intermediate target—that you may wish to utilize and blend into your routine.

Shot routines for putting and chipping are discussed in further detail later in this chapter.

Be sure to use the practice range to get your shot routine in good working order before using it on the course.

STANDING BEHIND THE BALL

You begin the shot routine by standing behind the ball, determining your target, and sensing the target picture. As you did in Chapter 4, you will sense the components of the target picture, including your intended ball flight path. This will induce the proper swing feel needed to react to your target picture and give you an idea of the proper club with which to make your swing. Learn to trust your instincts and to be honest with yourself.

Standing behind the ball, determining the target, and sensing the target picture

This is also the time to experience the benefits of a deep breath. Once you are standing behind the ball sensing your target picture, your routine has begun, and your attention should now be focused on the shot at hand. A deep breath at this time will help you relax, shut out the rest of the world, and heighten your awareness of the target picture.

ADDRESSING THE SHOT WITH TARGET AWARENESS

Now you are going to concentrate on the feel of the setup with regard to your intended ball flight path and the proper swing needed to react to the target picture. Again, there will be no mention of mechanics; those are to be worked out on the practice tee.

Notice the above heading reads "Addressing the *shot* with target awareness" and not "Addressing the *ball* . . ." The most important thing to learn is that the target picture controls the setup. You approach and set up to your intended ball flight path to the target, not just to the ball.

So, you have already sensed your target picture from behind the ball, including your ball flight path, and the proper swing feel necessary to react to that picture. You have also selected a club.

Now approach the shot. Still sensing the ball flight path, sole your clubhead lightly on the ground behind the ball and assume your stance. (If you don't wish to sole your clubhead, then just set it close to the ball and the ground.) Sense that the sweet spot of the clubface and the ball are one, as though the ball were actually bonded to the sweet spot of the clubface. Be careful, of course, not to actually touch the ball while you are sensing this.

Sole the clubhead lightly behind the ball.

This is the feeling that you are completely "measured up" to the shot; it can be felt at any point during the waggle or swing, not just when the clubface is in close proximity to the ball. (Find an old club and cement a ball to the sweet spot of the clubface as shown on page 101. Make full swings, at a normal pace and in slow motion, and sense this "oneness" throughout the entire swing motion. With practice this sense of oneness will become instinctive.)

While maintaining this feeling of oneness, rotate your head toward the target picture, so your eyes follow the direction of your upcoming swing path through the ball (see Chapter 6, Exercise 4), and continue sensing your intended ball flight path to the target. (Be sure not to raise your head and body

Feel the oneness between the sweet spot of the clubface and the ball.

Rotating your head toward the target picture

when you rotate your head, because this can distort or divert your target focus and possibly program you to "come over" the shot.) Now, while still maintaining a feeling of oneness between the clubface and ball, adjust the position of your body and club to allow yourself a swing that will propel the

Setting up to the shot with target awareness

ball along your intended ball flight path to the target. Then rotate your head back to the ball.

At this point you are fine-tuning the position of your body and club with respect to your intended ball flight path as you maintain a sense of oneness between the sweet spot of your clubface and the ball. You want to feel that the path the sweet spot of your clubface takes, as your swing reacts to your intended ball flight path, will just happen to pass right through the ball. *The feeling is that the ball will just be getting in the way of the clubface as your swing instinctively reacts to the target.*

If you have difficulty sensing the position of your body and club with respect to the ball flight path, return to the exercises in Chapters 5 and 6. If you still have difficulty, you may wish to utilize an intermediate target, as explained later in this chapter.

The key priority when addressing a shot with target awareness is to set up to the entire ball flight path of the shot and not just to the ball. While setting up to the shot you are always in motion, feeling and sensing your alignment with respect to your intended ball flight path. You will naturally flow into the next component of the shot routine, the waggle.

WAGGLING THE CLUB WITH TARGET AWARENESS

The waggle is a continuing movement of the body and club that occurs when you address the shot. It accomplishes many things: It magnifies and previews a definite pace of motion before the swing. It allows you to find your optimum balance to execute the shot. It lets you continue to instinctively fine-tune your sense of the alignment of your body, club, and swing path with respect to the target picture, including any instinctive adjustments necessary due to changes in wind direction or velocity. The waggle brings the setup to life, dynamically expressing the rhythm and feel of the impending swing to the target and allowing you to seamlessly flow through the forward press and into the swing.

In short, a correct waggle primes you for the shot, keeping your senses cognizant of, and your instincts ready to, your intended ball flight path to the target.

Not everyone has the same temperament, so not everyone waggles the club in the same fashion. The important thing is to sense the upcoming shot to the target in your waggle; and since golf shots vary widely, you don't want to groove your waggle.

How is it done? Watch some very good golfers—tour players, club professionals, and the better amateurs. Many of them have excellent waggles that are fluid, rhythmic, and simple. Watch Raymond Floyd as he goes through his shot routine and waggles the club. You can almost *see* him sensing the target picture and relating the feel of his body and club at address to that picture. By keeping his body in motion, he previews the rhythm of his swing and allows himself to flow right into the swing. In your quest for a good shot routine, there is no substitute for observing great players.

So, you are set up to the shot, feeling the position of your body and club with respect to your intended ball flight path as you maintain a sense of oneness between the sweet spot of your clubface and the ball. Next, move your arms very slightly—just an inch or two—back and forth behind the ball along the line of your intended swing path. This previews the path of your arms and club through impact. Along with the limited motion of your arms, let your wrists cock slightly as a small preview to how they will cock at the top of the swing. Let your weight shift slightly back and forth, from foot to foot, in a smooth and easy manner. The rhythm of the movements of your arms, wrists, and body previews the pace of your upcoming swing. Learn to preview the oily, fluid pace that you established in Exercise 6 of Chapter 6.

As you waggle, you may wish to rotate your head toward the target picture as before to facilitate sensing your intended ball flight path.

When you waggle, be sure not to raise the clubhead and pass it over the top of the golf ball. This motion hinders the feeling that the ball will just be getting in the way of the swinging clubhead, interrupts your sense of oneness between the sweet spot of the clubface and the ball, and causes you to raise your upper body, which could easily program your swing to "come over" the ball. Strive to only preview feelings in your waggle that you will use in your swing.

Let your grip feel light and alive, your wrists supple and fluid. Let your hands feel the weight of the club, and sense what their position will be at impact with respect to the target picture.

It is important to note that with just a little practice these movements of the setup and waggle will begin to take place instinctively as long as your awareness remains focused on the target picture.

The waggle with target awareness

It is at this point that your sense of the impending shot is at its peak. Through practice, you will be able to develop a strong connection before you swing between your body, the clubface, your swing path, and the intended ball flight path to your target. As you do you will develop an ever stronger feeling that the shot will take place exactly as you have sensed it would—indeed, that your intended result is the only possible result!

To review, throughout the setup and waggle you are sensing your intended ball flight path to the target and the position of your body and club with respect to it while maintaining a sense of oneness between the sweet spot of your clubface and the ball. You are also instinctively previewing the pace of your upcoming swing through the fluid movements of your body and club. After rotating your head to the target once or twice, along with waggling the club once or twice, you are ready to start the swing with a small motion called a "forward press."

THE FORWARD PRESS WITH TARGET AWARENESS

The forward press is the motion that triggers the swing. It is any motion from which you can softly rebound to begin the backswing. The chances are good that you already instinctively accomplish a forward press and that you need not further concern yourself with it. If you wish to, however, there are a few small movements from which to choose: you can "kick" your right knee in slightly toward the target; press your hands forward toward the target; or shift your weight slightly toward the target and then rock back away from the target to begin your swing. And there are others.

You may wish to rotate your head away from the target along the direction of your swing path, or perhaps firm up your left-hand grip with respect to the target picture. Whichever one you choose, be sure to do it with target awareness. This will maintain the awareness of your intended ball flight path right through the forward press and into the swing. And be sure that if you rebound into your backswing, you keep any increase in your grip pressure to a minimum.

THE SWING WITH TARGET AWARENESS

Your swing will be an instinctive reaction to your awareness of the target picture, so there's no need to think about anything, no need to consciously try anything. Just do it. Just

The swing with target awareness

swing. Simply trust your subconscious to do the right thing and let it be free and unencumbered to instinctively react.

If you do this (and it is not always easy at first), you will watch in amazement as your ball goes exactly where you sensed it should go. You will discover the power of the correctly programmed, unencumbered subconscious mind and the pure excitement of trusting it to react successfully.

AFTER THE SWING

There are two important things that you must incorporate into your shot routine that take place after the swing. First, understand that your shot, however good or bad, is not an indicator of your character, ability, luck, or what have you. In other words, don't overreact to it. Just stay in the present. Second, watch the flight of the ball until it stops moving—completely stops.

Watching the motion of the ball, no matter where it goes or how I struck the shot, has become my favorite part of golf. The way it really sails, or skids, and the effects of side-spin, gravity, and the terrain are things that I believe would fascinate more players if only they would take the time to look. Unfortunately, many golfers are too busy judging or rationalizing the results to really notice the flight and thus fail to watch the ball until it stops rolling. Next time out, make it a point to watch the ball until it stops rolling without judging the results. Observe how the ball conforms, or doesn't conform, to your intended ball flight path. Watch how it flies out of its lie, notice any effect from the slope of

Always watch the ball until it stops rolling.

the stance, observe what the wind does to it. When your ball lands, watch how it bounces, rolls, and comes to a stop, and notice how close you came, or didn't come, to your target.

If you want to react to the result of your target-oriented performance, go ahead—let it out and be done with it. But remember, if you don't keep your perspective about golf as a game, your anxiety and tension will increase, and so will your grip pressure, possibly activating the *hit* impulse.

You now know the individual parts of the shot routine with regard to the target picture, from beginning to end. Now, let's go through the entire shot routine to get an idea of how it flows.

One Flowing Routine

First, stand behind the ball. Determine the target and sense the target picture, including the ball flight path. Then sense the proper swing feel needed to react to the target and choose your club.

Approach the shot and, still sensing the ball flight path, place your clubface behind the ball and assume your stance. While maintaining a feeling of oneness between the sweet spot of the clubface and the ball, rotate your head back and forth along your intended swing path through the ball and adjust the position of your body and club to allow yourself a swing that will propel the ball along your intended ball flight path. Next, flow naturally into the waggle, sensing the feel and rhythm of the upcoming swing. As part of a continuing rhythm of motion, forward press and let yourself swing, trusting your subconscious to instinctively react to your awareness of the target picture. After the swing, watch the ball until it stops rolling.

The Imaginary Shot with Target Awareness (Heretofore Called a Practice Swing)

An imaginary shot with target awareness is a practice swing and much more. It's a practice swing married to a target picture; it's a preparatory swing for your real shot. You may want to include one in your shot routine, as it can be very useful. It gives you a chance to actualize the proper swing feel induced by sensing your intended ball flight path before you strike the shot. In doing so, you are further programming the way in which your subconscious will instinctively react during the swing

An imaginary shot gives you a sense of the weight and swing feel of the club you'll be using. It allows you to feel, and rehearse, the *swing* instinct, helping to alleviate any tendencies you may have to "hit at" the ball. Thus, it lets you preview the proper swing pace, which should have a greater feeling of motion from the ball on through. It gives you the sense, once again, that the ball is just getting in the way of the clubface as your swing reacts to the target picture. The benefits of incorporating an imaginary shot into your shot routine are considerable.

The purpose of the imaginary shot is not really to give

you a feel you can imitate when you play your real shot. It's just a way of previewing, or rehearsing, your subconscious instinctively reacting to the target picture.

To execute the imaginary shot with target awareness, briefly sense the flight path of an imaginary ball about twelve inches to the side of your real ball (its flight path should be virtually the same as for your real ball). Approach the imaginary shot and assume a stance. While maintaining a feeling of oneness between the sweet spot of your clubface and your imaginary ball, rotate your head back and forth along your intended swing path (through your imaginary ball) and adjust the position of your body and club to the target picture to allow yourself a swing that will propel the imaginary ball along your intended ball flight path. Next, waggle, forward press, and simply allow your swing to react to the target picture. Sense your imaginary ball flying on its intended flight path and then bouncing and rolling to a stop at your target. You have given yourself an excellent preview of the upcoming swing with the ball, and now it's time to instinctively play your real shot.

An important thing to note is that the execution of the imaginary shot is virtually the same as for the shot itself, and both should take place in a timely manner, without delay. If you incorporate an imaginary shot into your routine, be sure to work your routine out on the practice tee until it's one smooth, blended motion that you won't have to think about and *that won't slow down your play or the play of others.*

Setting up for the imaginary shot with target awareness

One Flowing Routine—
with an Imaginary Shot

First, stand behind the ball. Determine the target and sense the target picture, including the ball flight path. Then sense the proper swing feel needed to react to the target and choose your club.

Briefly sense the flight path of an imaginary ball about-twelve inches to the side of your real ball (it should be virtually the same as for your real ball). Approach and execute your imaginary shot. Sense your imaginary ball flying on its intended flight path and then bouncing and rolling to a stop at your target.

Approach your real shot and, still sensing the ball flight path, place your clubface behind the ball and assume your stance. While maintaining a feeling of oneness between the sweet spot of the clubface and the ball, rotate your head back and forth along your intended swing path through the ball and adjust the position of your body and club to allow yourself a swing that will propel the ball along your intended ball flight path. Next, flow naturally into the waggle, sensing the feel and rhythm of the upcoming swing. As part of a continuing rhythm of motion, forward press and let yourself swing, trusting your subconscious to instinctively react to your awareness of the target. After the swing, watch the ball until it stops rolling.

Utilizing an Intermediate Target

From the standpoint of alignment, the most important thing you do when you address a shot with target awareness is set up so that your upcoming swing will propel the ball along your intended ball flight path to the target. There is, however, an optical stumbling block in setting up to the proper direction of your intended swing path; it involves maintaining a correct sense of that direction while you approach the shot and take your stance. When golfers are at address for all shots except putts and chips, their eyes are well inside the line of their swing path through the ball. Hence, there is a

On this shot, the white eye-to-ground line is well inside the direction of the golfer's intended swing path through the ball.

*Selecting an
intermediate target*

tendency, if you are a right-handed golfer, to set up on a line that points to the right of the line on which you think you are aimed (lefties usually inadvertently aim left). There is an easy cure for this bit of optical confusion at address: selecting an intermediate target.

To use this technique—and it comes highly recommended—do the following: After you have visualized your intended ball flight path, and while you are still standing behind the ball, pick a spot 18 to 24 inches in front of the ball exactly on the line of your intended swing path through the ball. It can be a bent blade of grass, the edge of a divot, anything. Now you can set up to the direction in which you want to swing with dependable accuracy, because you have as a reference the imaginary line from your intermediate target back through the ball and continuing on behind the ball for a couple of feet.

Aligning yourself to the intermediate target at address. It is located on the white line, which is the direction of your swing path through the ball. The black line is your intended ball flight path.

However, you must be cautious, because the intermediate target is just a mechanical aid, serving only as a reference point to ensure that you get lined up correctly to your target picture. Once you have set up to that line, you must regain your instinctive sense of the target right away and feel your whole body and club positioned not just to the intermediate target, but to *your intended ball flight path to the target.*

One Flowing Routine— Using an Intermediate Target

First, stand behind the ball. Determine the target and sense the target picture, including the ball flight path. Then sense the proper swing feel needed to react to the target and choose your club. Select an intermediate target.

Approach the shot and, still eyeing your intermediate target, place your clubface behind the ball and assume your stance. While maintaining a feeling of oneness between the sweet spot of the clubface and the ball, rotate your head back and forth along your intended swing path through the ball (use your intermediate target) and adjust the position of your body and club to allow yourself a swing that will propel the ball along your intended ball flight path to the target. Next, flow naturally into the waggle, sensing the feel and rhythm of the upcoming swing. Use your intermediate target if you need to reverify the direction of your upcoming swing path, but again be sure that once you do so you return to sensing your intended ball flight path to the target. As part of a continuing rhythm of motion, forward press and let yourself swing, trusting your subconscious to instinctively react to your awareness of the target. After the swing, watch the ball until it stops rolling.

One Flowing Routine— with an Imaginary Shot and Using an Intermediate Target

First, stand behind the ball. Determine the target and sense the target picture, including the ball flight path. Then sense the proper swing feel needed to react to the target and choose your club.

Briefly sense the flight path of an imaginary ball about twelve inches to the side of your real ball (it should be virtually the same as for your real ball). Approach and execute your imaginary shot. Sense your imaginary ball flying on its intended flight path and then bouncing and rolling to a stop at your target.

Then go back behind the ball, briefly sense your intended ball flight path again, and select an intermediate target.

Approach the shot and, still eyeing your intermediate target, place your clubface behind the ball and assume your stance. While maintaining a feeling of oneness between the sweet spot of the clubface and the ball, rotate your head back and forth along your intended swing path through the ball (use your intermediate target) and adjust the position of your body and club to allow yourself a swing that will propel the ball along your intended ball flight path to the target. Next, flow naturally into the waggle, sensing the feel and rhythm of the upcoming swing. Use your intermediate target if you need to reverify the direction of your upcoming swing path, but again be sure that once you do so you return to sensing your intended ball flight path to the target. As part of a continuing rhythm of motion, forward press and let yourself swing, trusting your subconscious to instinctively react to your awareness of the target. After the swing, watch the ball until it stops rolling.

Your shot routine, from the moment you begin to sense the target picture, should take no more than 20 to 30 seconds. At first, you may feel as if you are being forced to swing before you are actually ready, but as you get adjusted to your routine this feeling will pass. *Always be attentive to determining your target and sensing your target picture while others are playing their shots.*

Be sure not to let any mechanical thoughts slip into your routine. If they do, you will invariably revert your focus back to the ball, with frustrating results.

Work on your shot routine for fifteen minutes daily on the range, at home, or in your mind, until you feel it's in good working order. Do not use it on the course until you have perfected it on the practice tee. Be sure not to waggle more than twice, and then just let your swing happen. In the long run, this is probably the most important exercise you can learn. Make sure you devote the time needed to getting it right.

Shot-Routine Variations for Putting and Short Shots

Putting and chipping generally require a slightly different routine because of the larger emphasis on rolling the ball along the terrain around the hole. Here, in addition to sensing the target picture from behind the ball, it can help to take a very brief look at the shot from another angle in order to better gauge the effect of the slope and speed of the green.

Moreover, since only a small arc and a negligible pivot are required for putting and chipping, you can choose to look at the target instead of the imaginary ball while making your imaginary putt (heretofore known as the practice swing or the practice putting stroke). This is a great technique to

Checking the slope of the putt from the side

better sense the path of the ball into the hole and the proper stroke necessary to react to that path. If you watch golf on TV, you may have noticed that several of the best players use it.

I believe that by keeping the mechanics of the putting stroke out of your mind, visualizing the ball going into the hole before striking the putt, and maintaining that awareness of your target during the putt, you will prevent or eliminate the "yips."

While there have been attempts, and even some limited success, at actually putting the ball while looking at the hole, I recommend that you look down toward the ball when making the stroke that will impact the ball.

Looking at the target picture while making an imaginary putt

Also, when golfers putt and chip, their eyes are much closer to being exactly over the direction of their intended swing path. This results in substantially less optical confusion at address, and it may not be necessary for you to utilize an intermediate target, even if you do use one with your full shots.

Be sure to go through your shot routine each time you play a shot. If you do, you will soon notice changes in your play. Your shotmaking will become more decisive and accurate. Stick with the shot routine until it truly becomes second nature; you'll be glad you did!

CHAPTER 8

Playing Golf with Target Awareness— Putting It All Together

Now it's time to play golf with target awareness. The first exercise is designed to allow you to let go completely. There is no substitute for this first experience of just letting go and trusting yourself.

Let go and swing

For this exercise, give yourself a good, level lie on the practice tee. Disregard all components of the target picture except the target and the ball flight path, and assume the ball flight path to the target will be a simple, straight trajectory. Take a 5-iron, sense the target picture from behind, and set up to the shot. Then, just swing. Totally let go of all your thoughts and conscious actions, except your awareness of the target, and just swing.

Can you do this? It is probably the simplest exercise of all, and yet it can be difficult at first. What you are doing is trusting your subconscious to perform correctly. When you address the shot, simply sense the target picture and swing. (If you have trouble sensing the target picture, repeat the exercises in Chapters 4 and 5.) Don't try to do anything during your swing, and don't think about anything—just sense the target and swing. You may want to try it with the ball on a tee. The secret is to maintain an awareness of your target, and your intended ball flight path, for the entire swing. Once you have done this correctly for one shot, you have accomplished the goal of this exercise.

LEARNING TO PLAY WITH TARGET AWARENESS

Now that you've felt what it's like to totally let go for at least one golf shot, you should take a more pragmatic approach. Repeat the previous exercise, starting with the short shots and working your way up to the long ones, building on success as you go. Begin with short putts, then putts of medium length, then long ones. Develop a feel for playing with target awareness on the green. Here, and with chipping as well, you can actually make your practice stroke while looking directly at your target. Take this opportunity to develop your feel on the green. Then move on to chipping and pitching. After you get to the maximum length that you strike your pitching wedge, move down through the irons, choosing appropriate targets with each club until you get to your longest iron. Then go to your woods, starting with the shortest club and working all the way up to the driver.

Always be sure to have a specific target and not just a direction, especially when playing the long shots. This keeps you from consciously trying to apply added force on the downswing that can ruin the shot.

Be sure to go through your shot routine each time, especially while practicing these shots on the range. Don't skip it in order to strike shots more quickly.

If you're playing the golf course and your game starts to leave you, don't immediately start analyzing the mechanics of your swing. Chances are you have just lost your target focus, and you may be able to get it back with a few target-aware practice swings like you learned in Chapter 5.

If you lose your target focus and find yourself unwittingly reverting back to the ball, after the round go back and do the drills in Chapter 6 for maintaining your focus throughout the entire swing. You may want to simplify your target picture by sensing just the target and the ball flight path to the target. And, if you're having trouble, always be sure to return to the shorter clubs, or a club you're confident with, to regain the proper swing feel.

Sometimes you may find that you just can't get a sense of the proper swing feel necessary to react to your target. When this happens, it may seem as if the shot "just doesn't set up for you." If your tendency is to draw the ball quite a bit, and you are on the tee of a sharp dogleg right with out-of-bounds on the left, a sense of the proper swing feel can be especially elusive. This is the time to go back behind the ball, imagine a new ball flight path, and come up with a new and different swing feel, one that completely disregards the previous target picture. In the example above, the golfer would have to know how to intentionally curve the ball from left to right. When a shot just doesn't instinctively set up for you, *create something new and different.*

Intentionally curving the ball left or right

I recommend curving the ball by just opening or closing your clubface at address and then making your normal swing. Like everything in golf, this requires some practice before you'll be able to instinctively adjust the alignment of your stance and clubface with respect to the target in order to start the ball on your intended flight path and obtain the proper amount of curvature. You must be very careful that you don't let the fact that the clubface is open or closed change the direction of your intended swing path. While practicing these shots or any others, always lay a club or two down on the ground and align them parallel with the direction you wish to swing for easy reference.

Intentionally curving the ball flight, and intentionally striking the ball high or low

Intentionally hitting the ball high or low

I recommend hitting the ball higher or lower by adjusting your ball position slightly forward for a higher shot, and back a little for a lower one. Again, only practice will give you the instinctive knowledge of how far to the front or back your ball position should be to give you the desired results. Be careful that you don't change your ball position so much that you lose solid contact with the ball when you swing.

Controlling the trajectory of shots to the green

If you succeed in gaining an instinctive feel for curving the ball, you may wish to consider setting up your shots to the

Controlling the trajectory of shots to the green

green in the following way. If the pin is left, aim for the center of the green with a little draw. If the pin is right, aim for the center of the green with a bit of fade. That way, if the curve doesn't happen you have the best chance of ending up in the safest part of the green, the center.

If the pin is in the front, play a higher shot that won't roll much and will tend to stay near the front of the green. If the pin is in the back, play a lower one to get a little more roll. You can have fun with these shots, and you will gain a lot of instinctive knowledge about how your setup can affect the ball flight path.

Keeping fit physically and mentally

Achieving success at playing golf in a target-oriented fashion is not that difficult, especially if you're willing to work at it. But to be successful over a longer period, to really gain some consistency with this method, you may have to make some changes in your lifestyle. For example, if you tend to rush around a lot before you play golf, doing errands and taking care of this or that, you may not be able to quiet your mind when you want to. Same goes for poor eating habits, excessive drinking, smoking, and not getting enough fresh air and exercise. Mental and physical well-being go hand in hand; therefore, to play golf with target awareness, you may need to cultivate a calmer, more worry-free lifestyle.

In my opinion, if you are interested in improving your golf game—and your life—you should regularly meditate and practice some form of yoga. Meditation is easy, you can do it virtually anywhere, and its benefits are tremendous. It quiets the mind and enhances awareness by decreasing the mind's constant inner conversation and chatter. It frees you up, prevents you from becoming too preoccupied with yourself, calms you, and tunes you in to the sounds of the world. Meditating twenty minutes every day is quite sufficient and will probably effect notice-able changes in your golf game.

Yoga is at once a form of meditation and physical exercise. When you practice yoga on a regular basis, you learn to *breathe correctly* and become calmer. Your balance improves, and so does your physical strength and stamina. And all the while you're continuing to increase your awareness and quiet your mind.

Next you'll examine how to improve your golf game through practice.

One of many yoga postures, called asanas

PART III

Practicing Golf

CHAPTER 9

Three Ways to Practice

Now that you've learned the proper way to play golf, it's time to learn how to practice.

There are three ways to practice golf. The first is to strike shots while thinking about one or more mechanical aspects of the swing. This is known as the *practice* mode. The second is to strike shots in your imagination. The third is to strike shots without making any conscious action during the swing and just letting your subconscious react to your awareness of the target. This is the *playing* mode. There is a correct time and place for each of these. Let's look at them in more detail.

Striking Shots While Thinking About the Mechanics of the Stroke

This method ingrains the various fundamentals, positions, and mechanics of the golf swing in your subconscious. It programs your subconscious so it can react on the course. It is important for golfers at all levels and is especially beneficial to those golfers with higher handicaps who need extra work on the fundamentals.

This type of practice should only be employed on the designated practice areas of your course or club, such as the practice tee, the practice green, or the putting green. It is best to practice in this manner after a round or during a general practice session when you won't be playing the course immediately afterward.

A good range with individual greens and flags as targets

There are five principles associated with this method.

One, never practice this way before a round of golf, and never practice this way on the golf course. Prior to the round, you just want to get a feeling for your entire swing rather than its individual parts. If you think about swing mechanics just before teeing off, you will most likely carry that type of thinking out on to the course. In Chapter 2 you learned how this can result in confusion and frustration.

Two, immediately follow any practice of this type with the third kind of practice, that of letting go of swing thoughts and letting your subconscious react to the target. You will thus end every practice session with your swing in one piece and your thoughts and feelings oriented toward the target, not the ball. No matter what you work on, or how minutely you dissect your swing, always finish your session with at least 10 to 20 target-aware swings—and no mechanical thoughts allowed!

If you practice diligently, the fundamentals you've been working on will become instinctive. But you can't force it. It takes a very large number of practice shots for a swing fundamental or a change to become fully ingrained in your subconscious.

Three, always have a target. Many of the older players were more target-oriented because they practiced with a live

Always lay a club or two down for alignment while practicing.

target, a caddie shagging balls, or they had to pick up the balls themselves!

Four, always lay one or two clubs on the ground parallel with the direction you wish to swing, to ensure correct alignment while you concentrate on other aspects of your shotmaking.

Five, always stay aware of your grip pressure. Too much tension in the hands will tighten your arms and upper body, restrict your swing arc, and impede the flow of your arm-swing. Your grip pressure should be firm enough so your hands stay unified and don't change position on the club while you swing, yet light enough so you don't have appreciable tension in your forearms. *Lightly firm, yet sensitive*, are words that some to mind. Most golfers tend to grasp the club too tightly and need to lighten their grip pressure.

Also, no matter how firmly you grip the club, you should strive to keep your grip pressure constant throughout the swing. See if you can keep it as close as possible to what it was at address. This will really help you keep conscious manipulation of the club out of your swing.

Just a few comments about this type of practice. Thinking about swing mechanics while striking shots- -being in the practice mode—is a great way to program the subconscious with the correct fundamentals of the golf swing. The good habits this promotes will give you a solid golfing foundation and put you on the path to a life full of golfing enjoyment. Be wary, however, for it is *incredibly easy* to develop bad habits in your golf game. And without competent supervised instruction, bad habits get worse, which leads to all sorts of golfing frustrations. *The secret to correctly learning the fundamental mechanics of the golf swing is to get plenty of supervised instruction from one or more qualified PGA professionals.*

You may want to augment your professional instruction by reading books written by certain successful golf instructors. Ask your instructor to recommend some books. I recommend *How to Become a Complete Golfer* by Bob Toski and Jim Flick with Larry Dennis; and *Shape Your Swing the Modern Way* by Byron Nelson with Larry Dennis.

These books will tell you all you need to know about the correct fundamentals of golf, and much more. They describe in detail the mechanics of the swing and provide plenty of drills expertly designed to enhance all your golfing skills, then they put it all together to show you how to apply what you've learned on the course.

Always keep in mind that you learn to crawl before you walk, and walk before you run. Learn to putt first, then proceed to chipping, pitching, and the longer shots. Always return to a shorter club when things go wrong.

Don't fall victim to offhand advice from friends and playing companions, or to the latest tips, tricks, and quick fixes from television shows and certain golfing periodicals. Seek out a competent PGA instructor, someone whose known success with students at your skill level will give you confidence in his or her teaching abilities. If possible, try to get your instructor to observe your game *on the golf course.* This is where he can really see what's causing you to shoot the scores you're shooting.

Go for long-term rather than short-term rewards. Give yourself, and your instructor, a chance for success. Stick with it. And, most important, *leave those mechanical swing thoughts on the practice tee.*

Striking Shots in Your Imagination

This is a great way to practice, and it can be done virtually anywhere. Can you picture a shot in your mind, then feel yourself execute that shot? If not a vivid shot, can you at least sense setting up to a shot and then feel yourself swinging back and through?

The ability to sense the proper swing feel needed to react to a particular target is a key part of learning to play target-oriented golf and, as you already know, a large part of what this book is about. It is a simple task that may prove a little difficult at first. You may sense a picture of the shot, but not be able to imagine yourself smoothly swinging the club back and forth exactly the way you'd like. The great thing about that is, what you can't do consciously in your imagination is very similar to what you cannot do physically with the golf club. So, if you earnestly practice the fundamentals of golf as mentioned above in the first type of practice, you will become better able to instinctively sense those correct swing fundamentals in your mind. Then, imagining yourself smoothly swinging the club back and forth, and picturing the ball as it follows your intended ball flight path, becomes easier.

Let's give it a try.

Picture and execute a successful shot in your imagination

Find a place where you can relax and sit quietly, and where no one will disturb you. You may want to close your eyes. Imagine you are at a place on your regular course, one you know well—say, a particular tee, fairway, or green—and go there. Perhaps it's the tee of a certain par 4. You are the only one around; you have the course completely to yourself.

Feel the sensation of taking your driver, or whatever club you normally use there, out of the bag. Sense the feel of the grip of the club in your hands. Sense the club's weight as you lightly hold it. Be sure to take extra time to feel every sensation in your mind as you proceed through your shot routine to your swing. Feel the shape and texture of the tee as you take it out of your pocket and tee up your ball. Can you smell the freshly cut grass? Feel a gentle breeze on your face? Stand behind the ball and locate exactly where you'd like the ball to finish. Then sense the target picture, including your intended ball flight path. Since you're familiar with the shot, you know exactly where you'd like the ball to finish. Feel yourself setting up to the shot and then waggling. Feel yourself swing back away from the target and through toward the target. Visualize the ball flying through the air, then landing and running right to the intended spot. Always picture a successful shot, not a poor one.

If you have trouble doing this exercise you may wish to think of one or two swing keys that will trigger the feel of a successful swing. Or, you may wish to physically swing a club with your eyes closed and review the various sensations. Feel the swing with the club a few times as you did in Exercise 5 of Chapter 5. Then *immediately review the feeling in your mind*. Swing the club a few more times and review the feeling again. If you're willing to devote some effort to this exercise, before long you'll be able to imagine the feel of smoothly swinging the club back and forth. *Do whatever it takes to sense the feel of executing a successful shot in your mind.*

PLAY A ROUND OF GOLF IN YOUR IMAGINATION

Once you are able to imagine the feel of executing good golf shots, use this skill to imagine playing a successful round of golf at your favorite course. Feel yourself on the first tee, making a successful shot to the desired spot on the fairway. Then feel yourself executing the swing that sends the ball right up next to the hole, or into the hole if you are so inclined. Why not? It's your imagination!

Continue feeling yourself make the shots you desire all the way around the course. This is similar to the visualizing exercise you did in Chapter 3, except now you are imagining the feel of executing the shots to those targets and not just sensing the intended ball flight path.

This is a great way to program your mind for success.

Striking Shots Without Making Any Conscious Actions During the Swing

This means, of course, striking shots with target awareness, which you have already begun to do. Practice this by repeating it over and over. Begin every shot by standing behind the ball. Complete your shot routine each time. Don't lose your target focus and revert to thinking about mechanics.

This type of practice can be done anywhere on the course grounds. It is called "practicing as you will be playing," or the playing mode, and is excellent for preparing your mind, body, and swing for the game itself. Make it your only method of practice before you play a round of golf. This way, you'll be able to take your game from the practice tee to the course with no change in your ability to strike good golf shots.

To make this practice more fun, you may wish to get competitive with yourself and see how many consecutive shots you can execute successfully. Or, you may wish to simulate an entire round on your course right there on the practice tee. Start with the driver then, depending on the result, calculate what your second shot will be and so on, through all eighteen holes. Finally, you may wish to go out on the course with a few balls to really get the feel of playing in a target-oriented fashion. Or invent something new. *Just be sure you put the method of making the stroke out of your mind and play with target awareness.*

How to Warm Up Before a Round

As mentioned previously, before a round you should only use the third type of practice, that of striking shots without any conscious swing thoughts, just reacting to the target. Make sure your shot routine is complete and moving smoothly. Feel the pace of your swing "from the ball on through," and stay tuned in to your intended ball flight path. This will enable you to preview how you'll be playing on the course and give you a genuine feel for just how you're swinging on that particular day.

Begin on the putting green by stroking a few long ones to establish your feel for the speed of the greens; follow this with some medium-length and short putts. Then you may want to stroke a few chip shots of varying lengths. Next, move to the range. Using the pitching wedge, start with half shots and work up to your full wedge shot. Get in touch with the fluidity of your swing by keeping your grip pressure light. Then move through the irons and woods at whatever pace you prefer, increasing the distance of your shots until you've used your driver. You may wish to end with the silky-smooth pace of a few sand-wedge pitches. Or, you may be content to finish with the club you'll be using on the first tee—probably the driver. Either way, a calm unhurried warm-up in the playing mode will help get your round off to a fine start.

Before touching a club, however, you should most definitely do a few exercises designed to loosen up your golfing muscles. The following six exercises only take about *three or four minutes* to do, yet their benefits are tremendous. *Always* take the time to do them.

If you don't have much time, the smooth pace of a few shots with chipping and pitching clubs will be much more beneficial than hurriedly whipping out the driver and blasting a few. The last thing you want to do before a round is preview a hurried, out-of-control swing pace. It is not worth the price of getting warmed up. Just stay calm and collected, and make an unhurried swing on the first tee. Then, while your companions are playing their shots to the first green, you'll be able to sneak in some of these warm-up exercises.

STRETCHING THE LEGS

By stretching the legs, you take pressure off the lower back, the single most injury-prone part of the golfer's body. If you incorporate these three stretches into your warm-up routine, you will significantly decrease the risk of lower back trauma. When doing any kind of stretching, never force anything, and always stop if you feel any pain.

Calf Stretch

This is a very common stretching exercise. With a club to hold for support, slowly and gently stretch your calf muscle in one leg. Repeat with the other leg.

Stretching the right calf muscle

Hamstring Stretch

Also a common stretch. While supporting your weight on one leg that's slightly bent at the knee, extend the other leg. Gently reach your hands toward the toe of your extended leg, or slowly bend forward from the waist. If necessary, use a club for support. Repeat with the other leg extended. You can also do this exercise by putting the extended leg up on the seat of a chair or bench.

Stretching the left hamstring muscle

Quadriceps Stretch

While balancing on one leg, hold the foot of your other leg against your buttocks by bending at the knee. Repeat with the other leg. If necessary, use a club, bench, or wall for support.

Stretching the right quadriceps muscle

STRETCHING THE TRUNK, SHOULDERS, AND NECK
The following three exercises get the rest of your body physically ready to swing the golf club.

Trunk Rotation

Put a club behind you, holding it in the crooks of your elbows, and assume your posture at address with your knees slightly flexed. Slowly turn to the right as you would for your backswing, and gently extend your turn as far as you can, stretching and limbering up the muscles in your trunk, shoulders, and neck. Keep looking toward where the ball would be while the rest of your body turns. Do the same in the other direction by turning all the way around to the left as you would for the finish of your swing. Repeat the entire exercise, turning both ways one or two more times.

*Trunk
rotation
with club*

Trunk and Shoulder Stretch

Raise your right elbow up near the top and back of your head and hold your right elbow with your left hand. Slowly and gently lean your upper body to the left, feeling the stretch up the entire right side of your trunk and shoulder. Do the same for the left side of your trunk.

Trunk and shoulder stretch

Swing two clubs at the same time

Take two long irons and swing them slowly and smoothly at the same time. Don't try to force it, just go along with the added weight and feel of the clubs. This is great for limbering up the golfing muscles and keeping them supple. Notice how light and easy it feels to swing one club, after swinging two.

Swinging two clubs at the same time

That's it! Do these six brief exercises, and you'll be on your way to getting warmed up and ready to play your best golf.

The goal of practicing is to gain an instinctive feel as to how to play a shot. You must be able to look at your game, see what part or parts you don't have an instinctive feel for, and practice them.

Look at your target game plan you created in Chapter 3. Note which kinds of shots you'll be playing more than others, and practice accordingly.

Always remember: whenever you practice, start with the shorter clubs and slowly work up to the longer ones. If you should momentarily lose the feel of your swing, return to a shorter club to regain it.

If you play right-handed and the wind on the range is blowing strongly from left to right, don't spend too much time out there striking full shots. That type of wind has a tendency to make you "come over" your shots, which can be harmful to your golf swing and practice intentions.

Lastly, be sure you understand the difference between the *playing* mode, in which you have no thoughts of swing mechanics and are letting your subconscious react to your awareness of the target, and the *practice* mode, in which you are thinking about swing mechanics. It is the crux of this book. *Always warm up by striking shots in the playing mode before walking on to the course.* You'll be able to take your game from the practice tee to the course with no change in your ability to strike good golf shots. You'll be ready to execute your shots swiftly and decisively and to enjoy the experience with an uncluttered mind. You'll be ready to *play* the game of golf!

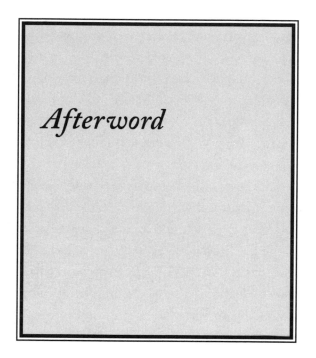

Afterword

Y ou will know you are well on the road to improving your game by playing golf with target awareness when you notice that the places on the course where your shots finish keep getting closer and closer to the targets you choose.

Consider the score a golfer would have if he or she played perfect golf. With a typical course having ten par 4s, four par 3s, and four par 5s, the total score for eighteen birdies would be 54. But the lowest possible score, ruling out double eagles, would be eighteen eagles, or a score of 36. No one has ever come close to a score of 50 for eighteen holes, let alone lower. In bowling a perfect game is 300, and it has been done many times. A perfect run to 125 has been achieved in national straight pool championship competition. Hence, compared to some other single-person sports, in golf there is still a lot of room for improvement.

I believe that target-oriented golf—trusting the subconscious to instinctively react to your awareness of the target picture—will be at the forefront of this improvement.

However, our society is not evolving in a way that's conducive to trusting the subconscious. We are, if anything, growing more analytical day by day. I believe there are two reasons for this.

First of all, we carry around a tremendous amount of internal chatter in our heads. We think and worry about everything we do, analyzing every move and justifying every action. This directly interferes with our ability to trust the subconscious to react. Consequently, we become separated from our instincts and are left with nothing but our analyses. As we get older, this internal chatter only seems to increase. We must learn to quiet our minds and allow our all-knowing subconscious to instinctively react without fear, without interference.

Secondly, the energetic conditioning of people in our society leaves little energy left over for target awareness in golf. It is the strength of our energy of awareness, contained in our energy body that exists along with our physical body, that determines the magnitude of our target sense. As humans we are all alotted just so much energy, and what we do with it literally determines our destiny. We humans, however, indulge more than any other species in activities that weaken our energy. Without the ability to focus our awareness on the target and hold it there, we give our subconscious little to react to. A strong target sense will help cut through a mind that chatters to itself, but a weak target sense and a chattering mind make it next to impossible to trust the subconscious to react properly throughout the entire swing. Again we come to that word *trust*. Consequently, while we learn to quiet our minds, we must look to new and different ways to reclaim and redistribute our energy of awareness, our target sense, and maintain it for longer periods of time. This can only be done by examining and changing certain modes of behavior in our daily lives. Only then will we be able to break through the present limitations in our scoring abilities and push the limits of the golfing envelope.